A BRIEF HISTORY OF WESTERN PHILOSOPHY

UNRAVELING THE SECRETS OF TIME, THE MIND, AND EXISTENCE

DOMINIC HAYNES

© **Copyright - Dominic Haynes 2022 - All rights reserved.**

The content contained within this book may not be reproduced, duplicated, or transmitted without direct written permission from the author or the publisher.

Under no circumstances will any blame or legal responsibility be held against the publisher, or author, for any damages, reparation, or monetary loss due to the information contained within this book. Either directly or indirectly. You are responsible for your own choices, actions, and results.

Legal Notice:

This book is copyright protected. This book is only for personal use. You cannot amend, distribute, sell, use, quote, or paraphrase any part, or the content within this book, without the consent of the author or publisher.

Disclaimer Notice:

Please note the information contained within this document is for educational and entertainment purposes only. All effort has been executed to present accurate, up-to-date, and reliable, complete information. No warranties of any kind are declared or implied. Readers acknowledge that the author is not engaging in the rendering of legal, financial, medical, or professional advice. The content within this book has been derived from various sources. Please consult a licensed professional before attempting any techniques outlined in this book.

By reading this document, the reader agrees that under no circumstances is the author responsible for any losses, direct or indirect, which are incurred as a result of the use of the information contained within this document, including, but not limited to, — errors, omissions, or inaccuracies.

CONTENTS

Introduction   5

1. Nature, Being, and Reality - The Pre-Socratic Ancient Greeks (600s - 300s BCE)   9
2. Out of the Cave - The Greek Giants (400s BCE - 535 CE)   27
3. The Age of Christian Ascendency - The Early Middle Ages (300s - 1200s CE)   53
4. A Pivot In the Late Middle Ages (1250 CE - 1500 CE)   77
5. Politics, Men, and Nature - The Renaissance (1400s - 1600s CE)   87
6. The Philosopher-Scientist: The Scientific Revolution and the Age of Enlightenment (1543 - 1815 CE)   101
7. Reason, Romanticism, and Ridiculousness in the Industrial Age (1815 - 1900 CE)   121
8. The Analytic and the Continental - Developments in Twentieth and Twenty-First Centuries (1900 - 2022 CE)   133

Other books by Dominic Haynes   161
References   165

HOW TO GET A FREE HISTORY EBOOK

Would you like a free copy of a surprise history ebook? Get free and unlimited access to the below surprise history ebook and all of my future books by joining my Fan Base.

Scan with your camera to join!

INTRODUCTION

'Every man bears the whole stamp of the human condition.'

— **MICHEL DE MONTAIGNE**

Once human beings advanced past the caves, the hunt, and the all-consuming need to survive, it wasn't long before questions about why they survived surfaced. As villages of mud and sticks morphed into cities of stone and bricks, men, both blessed and cursed by their intelligence, began to search for meaning in their existence, resulting in the development of various philosophies and religions.

Though philosophy will be the main subject, religion will be a frequent guest throughout this text since the two are so historically intertwined. Like sons of the same mother, the disciplines often grew together, influenced one another, and frequently diverged in opinion. However, both strove to answer the unquenchable question of why. Why do we exist? How are we meant to live? And what are we meant to do with our time here?

Philosophy, a Greek word meaning *love of wisdom*, encompasses many schools of thought from Eastern and Western traditions. It is difficult to separate the two since no one throughline of belief is endemic to either the Eastern or Western philosophers, though there do tend to be similar themes and ideas that recur. However, they can be divided by the geographical location of the philosophers and by the religions that influenced them. Thinkers who originated out of Europe and North America are classed as Western philosophers, while those native to Asia are considered Eastern philosophers. In the West, they were largely influenced by the pagan religions of Greece and Rome and the monotheistic traditions of Judaism, Christianity, and Islam, while religions like Buddhism and Hinduism had a greater impact on Eastern thought.

The focus here, as the title suggests, is the thinkers and ideas of the West. Much like the history of Western Civilization itself, this will begin with the Greeks, travel northward into Europe, and eventually cross the Atlantic into North America.

1

NATURE, BEING, AND REALITY - THE PRE-SOCRATIC ANCIENT GREEKS (600S - 300S BCE)

Around the 6th century BCE, Greece was growing into a powerful force, largely controlled by city-states like Athens, Corinth, Sparta, and Thebes. These societies, particularly the dominant city-state of Athens, developed social structures and a division of labor that allowed for a leisure class of scholars to exist. Without this development, the work of the philosopher-scholars of Greece would have been impossible.

The first Greek philosophers were mostly concerned with the physical world around them, searching for an explanation for the origin of the planet. Frequently called cosmologists or naturalists since the term "philosopher" didn't yet exist, these ancient men tended to espouse first monistic and later pluralistic ideas about the creation of the world. Simply put, those early philosophers believed that the world originated from either one singular source or substance (monism) or various sources and substances (pluralism).

As with much of ancient history, there's a good bit of fiction swirled in with the facts, and philosophy is no exception. The founders of philosophy in Greece are called the "Seven Sages" or "Seven Wise Men," but history cannot seem to draw a clear consensus on who these men were. First named by Plato (c. 428 - 348 BCE) in his work *Protagoras,* they are listed as Thales of Miletus, Pittacus of Mitylene, Bias of Priene, Solon the Athenian, Cleobulus the Lindian, Myson of Chenae, and Chilon of Sparta. However, Ephorus of Cyme, a historian, swapped Myson with a wise man from Scythia named Anacharsis while Demetrius of Phalerum replaced Myson with the tyrant of Corinth named Periander. This kind of substitution continued. Over the years, the first four names–Thales, Pittacus, Bias, and Solon–were typically always included, but the last three names were often changed depending on the source. Others included in the Seven Sages over time are Pythagoras, Aristodemus, Pamphylus, Epimenides, Leophantes, Acusilaos, and Scabras, to name a few. Sometimes religious pioneers like Orpheus, Linus, and Epicharmus might be folded in, but on the whole, it is Thales, Pittacus, Bias, Solon, and Pythagoras who are credited with the early development of Greek philosophy.

Most of the men listed above are now nothing more than names in a book; not much remains of their thoughts and contributions to history. However, the contributions of Thales of Miletus–often credited as the first Greek philosopher–have not been lost to time. Though none of his writings survived, he has a sterling reputation which speaks to his importance. Lauded in the field of mathematics, Thales utilized knowledge from the Babylonians to solve practical everyday problems - like calculating distance or height. He was also credited with achievements in the field of astronomy, like recommending navigation by the Ursa Minor constellation rather than Ursa Major. Though the two constellations are near one another, Ursa Minor contains Polaris–the North Star–making it more accurate for navigation than Ursa Major. Thales is also said to have predicted an eclipse, but whether or not he is truly responsible for all these intellectual feats is unknown.

In the field of philosophy, Thales is credited as the first person to offer a natural explanation for the creation of the world. Prior expositions on Earth's creation often included various mythical elements and involvement from the pantheon of Greek gods and goddesses.

Instead, Thales offered a story that was derived from the facts of the day. Sea fossils were discovered decently far inland at the time, so Thales hypothesized that everything on the planet had come out of the water, rather than out of the hands of various capricious deities.

One of his students, Anaximander of Miletus (610 - c. 546 BCE), attempted to create a slightly more elaborate origin story. Rather than water, Anaximander said that the world developed out of something called *Apeiron*, an entity that is simultaneously infinite and indistinguishable. Inside the *Apeiron*, the opposing forces of hot and cold arose. The struggle between these two contrasting entities created the entire world. Cold created the land and the sea while hot was responsible for the air and the mists. Hot also created rings of fire that surround the known universe. He thought that the Earth, though enveloped by mists, has small breathing holes that allow its inhabitants to see bits of the fiery rings. What is seen through these "breathing holes," according to Anaximander, are the sun, the moon, and the stars.

Building off of Thales' assumption that life came from water, Anaximander attempted to create a clear picture of how different animals developed. He asserted that all creatures that live on land must have an ancestor from the sea. He also believed that everything in creation would eventually return to the nebulous *Apeiron* from which it came. Finally, Anaximander realized that up and down were not absolute categories, and was the first to conclude that "up" referred to any direction away from the center of the Earth while "down" denoted the opposite. This meant that the Earth, in contrast to Thales' beliefs, did not need to be externally supported.

A third man from Miletus, Anaximenes (d. 528 BCE), believed that rather than water, the air was the source of all life. Unlike Thales and Anaximander who had no clear reason for how life appeared out of water or *Apeiron*, Anaximenes offered a process through which life could have arisen out of the air. He believed that matter came into existence when air changed its form through two methods: condensation or rarefaction. Condensation is the process through which the air becomes denser and more concentrated. According to Anaximenes, condensation would give rise to solid objects like earth or stone. In contrast, rarefaction would make the air thinner and purer, eventually leading to things like fire.

Though Thales had simply been searching for an explanation for the world or an *arche*–a Greek word meaning beginning–the work of Anaximenes transformed Thales' early thoughts into underlying principles. As a result, the very word *arche* took on the additional meaning of "principle." Naturally, the concept of an eternal principle is quite fundamental to philosophy in general and even though Anaximenes likely didn't quite realize what he contributed to the field, its importance remains. Eternal principles or *arches* are the foundational underpinnings of most philosophical thought.

These first three philosophers–Thales, Anaximander, and Anaximenes–were exceedingly ambiguous. Their philosophies did not sort matter into categories. Physical and emotional qualities were regularly intermingled. For example, heat and cold were interchangeably used as physical descriptors and emotional adjectives (i.e., love is warm and hate is cold). However vague their thoughts were, they were foundational to later, more clearly articulated Greek philosophy.

Building off of the work of the three Milesians, Xenophanes (c. 570 - c. 478 BCE), a traveling poet from the small town of Colophon, attempted to add more definition to their philosophies, particularly that of Anaximenes. Though many disregard Xenophanes as an artist or a theologian since much of his writing does not provide rational justifications alongside his claims, his thinking was influential for those who would follow. Thus, his writing and ideas are worth including in the history of philosophy.

Xenophanes was one of the first Greeks to actively criticize Greek religion. He argued that people tend to anthropomorphize deities, blaming them for all manner of calamities. He notes in Fragment 11 of his writing:

> *Homer and Hesiod have attributed to the gods*
> *All sorts of things which are matters of reproach and censure among men:*
> *Theft, adultery, and mutual deceit.*

Over the years, some have insisted that he instead espoused the idea that there is one eternal God, one ruler of the universe out of which all things flow. Others disagree, believing that he was simply against the practice of assigning human qualities to divine beings. It is difficult to view Xenophanes' work without a present-day lens, but at the time, monotheism was not viewed as all-important as it is to a Christian, a Jew, or a Muslim. To put it simply, he supported the idea that nothing can come out of nothing, and clearly, things exist in the world. This means that there must be an eternal "something" out there–some source of life.

Though not all philosophers and historians agree, this thought process formed part of the early foundations of Eleaticism. The founder, Parmenides of Elea (born c. 515 BCE), is often referred to as a student of Xenophanes, but this has never been fully verified. Frequently credited as the "Father of Metaphysics," he also is renowned for his deductive reasoning which places him second only to Aristotle (384-322 BCE) as the "Father of Logic."

For Parmenides specifically, much of what is known of his belief comes from fragments of his lengthy poem *On Nature* (the title is disputed) that were preserved by later figures, notably, Plato. The original work is thought to be eight hundred verses long, but only one hundred and sixty or so have survived. The fact that Parmenides' writing is quoted by later luminaries like Plato lends weight to his historical relevance, even if knowledge of the man's true belief system seems a bit thin in the present day. Nevertheless, he is the creator of the Parmenidean principle that "all is one," which is the basic belief system underlying Eleaticism.

Most Eleatics embraced Parmenides' general theory but tended to tweak it, add to it, or find different methods of proving it. For example, one of Parmenides' most notable students, Zeno of Elea (c. 495 - c. 430 BCE), credited by Aristotle as the inventor of the dialectic, used roundabout methods to prove Parmenidean principles. Parmenides himself preferred to use straightforward tactics whereas Zeno enjoyed the infinite regress and *reductio ad absurdum* methods to prove Parmenidean ideas. This "argument to absurdity" is a logical premise that aims to demonstrate that the opposing idea, if carried out, would lead to either a contradiction or ridiculousness. Zeno used this process to show that believing in the plurality of things rather than supporting the Parmenidean thought that "all is one" had fundamental logical inconsistencies.

Generally speaking, Eleaticism or the Eleatic School refers to a class of pre-Socratic philosophers who assert that everything in the world is one constant immovable thing. It is a particularly radical form of monism because rather than believing that everything comes from one source like water or air, Eleaticism espouses the idea that everything *is* one thing. Like Xenophanes, Eleatics believed that nothing can come out of nothing, so everything that humans perceive as coming, existing, and passing away is all a matter of perspective. To an Eleatic, reality is unchanging and contained in one "Being;" everything else like change or motion is just an illusion.

Eleaticism was developed primarily as a reaction to the other primary schools of thought at the time. One, which has already been covered a bit, was the empirical methods that led to the philosophies of the earlier Milesians. Thales and his compatriots embraced an observational mindset, preferring to base their philosophies on what they could fundamentally understand with their senses. Obviously, in contrast, Eleaticism involves a little bit of faith. Humans perceive the world as being made up of multiple things, all in motion. An Eleatic would ask you to suspend those sensory observations and acknowledge that all the things you can see and all the motion in the world around you are simply a grand illusion. It is an abstract, logical thought process to arrive at an Eleatic philosophy rather than one grounded in sensory perception.

Secondarily, Eleaticism differed on an ontological level from two other predominant ways of thinking. Ontology, in a very basic definition, is the philosophical study of being, becoming, reality, and existence. As stated earlier, Eleatics believed that everything is actually one thing that is defined by what it is. In contrast, some believed that a being is defined not only by what it is but by what it is not. This way of thought would later be elaborated by Plato. Furthermore, the philosopher Heraclitus, who was a contemporary of the most prominent Eleatics, thought that a being's essence or existence was defined and shaped by its interactions with its opposing force (i.e., hot and cold or light and darkness).

Eleaticism was strictly monistic. There was only the Eleatic One. Though it remained a popular philosophy, it was, as demonstrated above, hardly the only way of thinking at the time. Plenty of pluralistic philosophies were proliferating, but they were all deeply influenced by the thought process of Parmenides. Yet, despite the impact that Parmenides had on the field of philosophy, his idea of one singular being, the crux of Eleaticism, eventually fell out of favor when later thinkers like Plato and Democritus argued that if one "Being" exists, so then does its opposite: "Not-Being." For there to be something, there must be nothing to contrast it. Moving forward, the influence of Parmenides can be seen in pluralistic philosophers attempting to grapple with his esoteric idea that nothing is created or destroyed.

Empedocles of Acagras (c. 492 - 432 BCE) was one such pluralist. He claimed that all things consist of four main elements which he dubbed "the roots of everything." These substances are then mixed and separated by two forces–love and hate, respectively. Love and hate, in Empedocles' eyes, were eternal forces that had always existed and would always exist. They, in turn, randomly shape material things into living beings that come into existence and then pass away. A peer of his, Anaxagoras (c. 500 - c. 428 BCE), had a similar idea, but instead of love and hate, there was one force that set the particles of the universe in motion: *nous* or intelligence. However, unlike Empedocles, who believed that love and hate were blind forces acting at random, Anaxagoras taught that *nous* had a greater insight. In his mind, *nous* knew that by setting the particles in motion, all kinds of creatures would arise, but it refused to interfere once everything had begun. This is similar to the thought process that would later arise among Christian thinkers in the Enlightenment like Voltaire who saw God as a clock-maker that simply set the world in motion.

The most eloquent answer to the problems posed by Parmenides came first from Leucippus (5th c. BCE) and was further fleshed out by Democritus (c. 460 - c. 370 BCE). Though not much is known about him and some doubt his very existence, Leucippus is credited as the founder of atomism. Simply put, this is the idea that the universe is either empty space or filled space, and all things within the filled space are made up of atoms. Unlike the atoms of modern physics, Leucippus regarded atoms as the indivisible units of life–they can never be split. Much like the Eleatic One, Leucippus' atoms were neither created nor destroyed, but rather combined and recombined to create all the creatures and objects contained within the universe.

Though Leucippus remains a somewhat mysterious figure, historically speaking, more is known about his associate and supposed student, Democritus. Often referred to as the "laughing philosopher" due to his tendency to value cheerfulness, Democritus is also credited as a founder of atomism and is one of the most important pre-Socratic philosophers. Furthermore, if, as some assert, Leucippus never existed, then the ideas credited to Leucippus above would belong to Democritus alone. He was the first to suggest that the view of the Milky Way from Earth was a natural phenomenon and not the work of the gods. He is thought to have written over sixty different works on subjects as vast and varying as botany, ethics, musical theory, and physics, but very little of that canon of work has survived into the present day. Much of what we know and credit to Democritus comes from later philosophers who he influenced, most notably, Plato and Aristotle.

Democritus sought to illustrate how atoms worked in the physical world. He posited that certain objects are heavier or lighter because they contain more or fewer atoms, and also theorized that atoms congeal together to create objects or creatures via hook-like structures.

He extended this into ethical and moral ideas; if an individual is a good person, he is, quite literally, "well-composed." Meaning that the atoms that make up this person are put together well. He posited that violent actions or extreme passions can be destructive to a person's literal atomic composure, but this can be remedied through proper education.

He was also able to explain death with his atomic theory, believing that the soul was made up of fire atoms while the body was composed of earth atoms. When the soul left the body in death, the earth atoms could not keep their cohesion without the fire atoms, hence the body would decay and the atoms would disperse. Democritus' atoms have no qualities. They are not hot, cold, dry, wet, sweet, or bitter. Rather, they have only quantities that allow them to form different materials: a shape, an arrangement, and a position. Any qualities that humans experience are a result of the atoms interacting with their bodies, not because of any inherent wetness, coldness, or sweetness in an atom.

Aristotle, the chief source of any modern-day knowledge of Democritus, believed that atoms were simply reincorporated into a new form after dispersing out of an old one. Aristotle explains Democritus' theory using the alphabet. There are a finite number of letters, but they can be combined and recombined to form all the different words in a given language. New letters aren't needed for new words, just as new atoms are not needed for new forms.

Democritus is important not just for his influence on Aristotle and Plato, but also for his later influence on 17th-century thinkers like René Descartes. His weight is also felt in the field of physics since he was the first to correctly assert that the universe was composed of atoms.

The last pre-Socratic thinker of import lay outside the philosophical developments that began with Thales of Miletus. Pythagoras (c. 500 - 580 BCE), well known by geometry students everywhere, was a highly influential thinker and a huge source of inspiration for Plato, Aristotle, and every western philosopher who followed in later years.

Today, he is best known for his contributions to mathematics via the Pythagorean Theorem, though many historians suspect that this is a methodology Pythagoras borrowed from Babylonian thinkers. It has also been put forth by contemporary historians that much of Pythagorean thought is owed to either Babylonian or Egyptian ideas that he picked up during his travels. A contemporary of Xenophanes of Colophon and Heraclitus, his beliefs seem to slant more toward the mystical than either of those men. The former mocked Pythagoras for his belief in reincarnation while the latter simply considered him overrated.

Though notably tight-lipped about his teachings–he swore his disciples to secrecy–there are some basic tenets of Pythagoreanism that survived. Pythagoras believed that the soul was immortal and that it could move in and out of different animals over many different life cycles. Plato picked up on this idea, discussing in his book *Meno* that what is learned in life is simply the soul remembering what was learned in its former life. This concept, though hardly revolutionary in Eastern thought, was certainly novel in the West, hence the derision from Pythagoras' contemporaries. He is described as being quite ascetic, abstaining from sex, and eating a strict vegetarian diet (although Diogenes Laertius characterizes him as a pescatarian). His goal with these stern measures was to free himself from physical distractions to focus on the perfection of his soul.

Likely, much of his belief system was simply re-packaged Egyptian thought, but his pursuit of vegetarianism, pacifism, kindness to animals, and wish for inner peace was very different from the cerebral musings of his predecessors and peers.

Aside from his cultural contributions, from a purely scientific and philosophical aspect, Pythagoras was also revolutionary. He believed that "all things are numbers," and he attempted to find the structure and nature of things through numerical means. Some examples of this number theory include using numerical ratios to produce harmonies through different instruments or observing the mathematical predictability of the movements of the sun, moon, and stars. Math, for Pythagoras, was a path toward some ultimate truth or state of enlightenment.

Although it is not frequently realized by the general public, which readily credits Plato and Aristotle as pillars of Western Philosophy, if it hadn't been for the musings of Pythagoras, there would be no Plato. Without Plato, a large portion of Western Philosophy, including a great bulk of Christian teachings, falls apart.

2

OUT OF THE CAVE - THE GREEK GIANTS (400S BCE - 535 CE)

During the middle of the 4th century BCE, there was a change in Greek philosophy. The champions of this new thought process were wanderin teachers who charged a fee for the privilege of learning from them. This was a sharp departure from previous philosophers. Alongside charging money to instruct the wealthier classes of Greece in *aretē* (meaning virtue or excellence), these men also had a more realistic outlook on the world in general.

These Sophists, as they were called, saw little point in the idle musings of philosophers if they had no import on day-to-day life. As notable Sophist Protagoras of Abdera (c. 490 - c. 420 BCE) quipped, "man is the measure of all things, of those which are that they are, and of those which are not what they are not." Essentially, what Protagoras and other Sophists argued was that man sees and experiences the world a certain way. What is the point of arguing about things we cannot see, taste, smell, or experience? If one person feels cold but their friend insists that it is hot, does that change the fact that that person still feels cold?

Gorgias, another Sophist and a younger peer of Protagoras, was famed for his oratory skills and use of rhetoric. His famous work *On That Which Is Not* (or, *On Nature*) argues that nothing actually exists but even if something did exist no one would know or be able to communicate that knowledge to another person. Essentially, even though many believe that his work has a mocking or satirical tone, Gorgias was hinting at the subjective nature of the human mind. Everyone's realities are slightly different due to differing perceptions of the world around them. Though his work fell out of favor after Plato was critical of him in his dialogue *Gorgias*, his work was later influential to European relativists in the 19th century.

Generally speaking, the Sophists were skeptical and critical of the world, not just prior philosophical teachings. They equally looked askance at cultural traditions surrounding sex, marriage, burial, and the general societal code of conduct that was expected at the time. They were more interested in being successful and influential, gaining power and wealth by convincing those around them to follow their lead. However, it should be noted that many of the characterizations of Sophists stem from Plato's dialogues, and he was not particularly fond of them or their work. Even the modern definition of the word sophistry includes the use of fallacious arguments with the active intent to deceive.

Thus, it is surprising that this next man is sometimes lumped in with the Sophists, even though he espoused some major departures from his supposed colleagues. Socrates (c. 470 - 399 BCE) did not teach for money and lived a relatively frugal life. His philosophies mostly dealt with seeking universal truths and goodness while typical Sophists were more interested in relativity and subjectivity. Perhaps Socrates started more closely aligned with Sophist values, but he is likely only associated with them due to their proximity in history.

Additionally, the term Sophist did not gain its derisive cast until later. In earlier times before the term philosopher was adopted, a Sophist simply referred to a wise man. With the word philosopher reaching the popular lexicon right around the rise of Socrates, it is also possible he was referred to as a Sophist since it was initially somewhat analogous to philosopher. After all, the term Sophist arises from the Greek words for wise and wisdom; *sophos* and *sophia*, respectively.

As for Socrates himself, what is known of him is known only through his disciples. He did not instruct or write, but rather he engaged in open dialogues in public. The question-and-answer style of teaching known as the Socratic method arises from his practice. He was known for engaging with anyone, regardless of age or social class, and was mostly interested in delving into the inconsistencies between people's thoughts, beliefs, and actions. His life philosophy was two-fold: firstly, one should never, even indirectly or inadvertently, do wrong and secondly, once one knows what is right and good, one should never act against it.

There are many examples of Socrates living out these two principles in his own life, like the time he refused to condemn an admiral to death without a trial following the Battle of Arginusae (406 BCE). The majority of the Athenian assembly exhorted him to do so, but Socrates, who happened to be in charge of the assembly that day, flatly rejected them. He remained stalwart in his stance, despite receiving threats from the general populace. Socrates was openly critical of some aspects of democracy, fearing it could easily devolve into mob rule.

In 404 BCE, democracy in Athens was overthrown when the Spartans imposed an oligarchy on the city-state during the aftermath of the Peloponnesian War. Known as the Thirty Tyrants, these men, led by Critias, were considered extremist and oppressive. With a strong conservative bent, they began to purge the city of those who did not fall in line, killing as many as 1,500 people. The Tyrants attempted to coerce all citizens of Athens into participating in their mayhem, but Socrates, understanding the danger but believing it to be wrong, simply refused.

As previously mentioned, Socrates loved to identify and point out inconsistencies in people's beliefs and behaviors. One he was particularly fond of highlighting was that a person will often laud heroic actions in others but refuse to live them out in his own life. For example, dying for one's beliefs is looked upon with reverence, but most people will do anything to avoid being that person. Conversely, being cowardly is frequently mocked and derided, but many people, given the chance, will be cowardly to preserve their own lives. Socrates' ability to pinpoint hypocrisy earned him a fair bit of praise and admiration, but it also fostered bitterness and irritation among those whom he exposed, particularly people in power.

Eventually, his detractors caught up with him. After Athenian democracy was restored, Socrates was charged with corrupting the youth of Athens and behaving immorally. Now, history believes these charges to be completely false and essentially an excuse for the powerful in Athens to be rid of Socrates. His trial is characterized as a devastating example of democracy gone awry under mob rule. However, again it should be noted that the sources available in the present day are likely quite biased towards Socrates since most sources stem from his students and admirers. Greek and Athenian morals and politics are different from present-day beliefs, and he may have been fairly charged and convicted when looking at the event through the eyes of an ancient Athenian. Ultimately, he was condemned to death and as Plato tells it, in 399 BCE he drank hemlock poison to end his life.

Yet, despite the Athenian authorities' best efforts, Socrates' influence reached far beyond the grave. He became a dominant figure in philosophy during the Greek and Roman times, and he has remained so ever since. Though he never wrote his philosophies down into great treatises, his way of thinking was preserved and passed down through his adherents. Plato and the historian Xenophon wrote Socratic dialogues, others, like Eucleides of Megara, Antisthenes, Diogenes of Sinope, and Aristippus of Cyrene founded their own schools and sects that were deeply influenced by Socratic thought.

Eucleides, the founder of the Megarian School, tended to emphasize Socrates' more theoretical ideas, espousing the Socratic question-and-answer method. Antisthenes and his pupils skewed more towards Socrates' tendency to eschew material things. This impulse was further magnified under Diogenes of Sinope, the founder of the Cynics. These men took the idea of austerity to the extreme, believing that everyone should be free from not only material greed but also societal conventions. Finally, Aristippus of Cyrene, the originator of the Cyrenaic school, took a more laid-back approach. He agreed with the previously mentioned philosophers that desiring and chasing after material goods was a bad idea, but he said people should be able to acquire these things and live a comfortable life as long as they are apathetic about losing them. Eventually though, the Cyrenaic school took on a decidedly more hedonistic bent, preaching that pleasure was the only good to be found in life.

Despite the multifarious schools of thought and ways of life that erupted after Socrates' demise, it was one student, Plato, who would prove to be the most influential one over time. Born in Athens to a noble family whose lineage can be traced back to the ancient kings of Athens, he deeply admired Socrates, even though he came from a simpler background and upbringing. He was a young man during the turbulent Peloponnesian War and the ensuing political upheaval wrought by the rule of the Thirty Tyrants. Though hopeful that things would improve politically once democracy was restored in Athens, young Plato was quite disillusioned with the whole process after witnessing what he believed to be the corruption and demagoguery that led to Socrates' execution. As a result, he believed, quite opposite from his mentor, that philosophers should absolutely be involved in political institutions.

He elaborated on this idea in the *Republic*, arguing that political leaders should become philosophers or vice versa. He notes:

> The society we have described can never grow in to reality or see the light of day, and there will be no end to the troubles of the states, or indeed...of humanity itself, till philosophers become rulers in this world, or till those we now call kings and rulers really and truly become philosophers, and political power and philosophy thus come into the same hands.

Plato's concept of "philosopher-king" would echo through Europe with many rulers striving to emulate the mold laid out by Plato. Historically speaking,

Alexander the Great of Macedonia and Emperor Marcus Aurelius of Rome are often pointed to as exemplary examples. Interestingly enough, Alexander the Great was educated in his youth by Aristotle, one of Plato's students.

Saddened by the state of affairs in Athens, Plato briefly left the city for a stint in southern Italy, only to be met by worse corruption and tyranny in the town of Syracuse. Eventually, he wound his way back to Athens and opened the Academy; an institution meant to educate philosophers. He continued to write Socratic dialogues, encapsulating what he remembered of his departed teacher, but he also wrote his oeuvre, the *Republic,* right around the same time.

In this text, Plato lays out the ideal state. While it might be surprising for a Greek thinker to reject democracy as the consummate political structure, Plato does just that. He argues that all the ills of humanity essentially boil down to an inability to govern and control one's passions. As a result, the perfect state would be ruled by an elite, highly educated class and supported by a strong warrior class to enforce it. The rulers would live austere, barren lives, with no possessions and no family. Thus, free from the distractions of the world, they could govern fairly and impartially. The ruling class would be supported economically by the working class, who are, in turn, permitted to enjoy life's pleasures, own personal belongings, and have a family.

Plato and one of his adherents, Dion, attempted to bring this ideal state into reality in Syracuse during the reign of Dionysius II, but this was a failure. In later works, notably *Statesmen* and *Laws,* Plato would lament that due to the failings of human nature, only a god could faithfully execute absolute power over a people. To keep human rulers in check, rigid rules were needed.

Aside from his real-world political dealings, Plato also had many contributions to theoretical philosophy; the most memorable being his theory of Forms. In his Socratic dialogues, when Socrates is questioning someone, digging into their inconsistencies, he would often ask the individual what made an action or a person a certain kind of quality (brave, beautiful, or good, for example). Unable to satisfactorily answer this, Plato began to posit that there is some kind of indefinable idea (*eidos*) that a person has of good, brave, or beautiful. Plato wanted his audience to realize certain qualities in life do not have a tidy definition.

This was taken further when Plato made the mathematical discovery that no two things are truly, perfectly equal, just as nothing is perfectly good or perfectly brave. Yet, all these ideas–equality, goodness, beauty, courage-are all basic components of human life. He believed that there must be another realm beyond the senses, a world of eternal Forms, where the perfect versions of everything exist. Things that are seen in the world of the senses are simply imperfect copies of the world of perfect Forms. The classic example often used is a chair. There are many chairs in the world that all look different and function slightly differently, but in the world of Forms, there is the original perfect chair from which all other chairs derive their general likeness and inspiration.

To Plato, the most important thing in this realm of Forms was Good, which trumped both being and knowledge. Note that being in this context is meant to describe an actual being, like a person or an animal. He noted in the *Republic* during his famous *Allegory of the Cave* that human knowledge begins with the world of the senses, observing and learning about what can actually be seen, smelled, heard, touched, or tasted, and progresses into the realm of the Forms.

Plato, unlike his mentor, died of old age in Athens, leaving behind many valuable works of writing and his educational institution, the Academy, intact. His Academy would continue to operate for centuries after his passing. Arguably though, aside from his myriad of written works, Plato's most enduring contribution to philosophy came in the form of his student, Aristotle.

Born in 384 BCE in Stagira, a seaside town on the eastern Greek peninsula of Chalcidice, Aristotle is considered an intellectual giant in Western history. His work served as a skeleton for much of the Christian philosophy and theology in medieval Europe and a framework for medieval Islamic thought. Despite the multitude of scholars who came after him, Aristotelian philosophy still forms much of the underlying thought in Western cultures. He contributed to biology, physics, chemistry, and countless other fields, but he is chiefly known for his establishment of formal logic and his efforts in the study of philosophy.

Eventually, Aristotle made his way to Athens and at age 17, began to study at Plato's Academy, though Plato himself was in Sicily at the time. Following Plato's death, his nephew Speusippus took charge of the Academy, and Aristotle left Athens. Traveling first to Assus in Anatolia, he then spent some time on the island of Lesbos before receiving a summons to the Macedonian court in Pella. Appointed to educate the young crown prince, Alexander–who, as was mentioned earlier, went on to become the famed philosopher-king, Alexander the Great–Aristotle resided in Pella until Alexander himself ascended to the throne. With Alexander no longer needing his tutor, Aristotle returned to Athens where he founded his own school, the Lyceum.

Though it is debated to what extent, at some point during his twenty years at the Academy, Aristotle began forming his own philosophical thoughts. What is known is his disagreement with portions of Plato's theory of Forms. He did not agree with the idea of a realm of perfect, transcendent forms. Rather, he argued that the world humans perceive is the real world and that to build knowledge and understanding about certain groups of things in the world (e.g. groups of plants), some things can be held "generally" true about these groups. So, instead of holding fast to the idea of perfect Forms, Aristotle believed that there are general qualities that human beings can observe and hold to be true.

Additionally, like Plato had developed an idea of a supreme Good that occupied the highest place in his hierarchy of forms, Aristotle too had a thesis on the origins of the universe. He believed there was a prime mover, or "unmoved mover," that was the impetus for all motion. This entity was immortal and unchanging, able to move all things but remain unmoved. This, as will be explored later, was hugely influential in medieval Christian doctrine.

Aristotle built on and adapted Plato's ideas further in his teleology or "doctrine of purposiveness." He believed that instead of an idea of perfection existing in another realm, everything in the sensory world is on a journey to perfection. That is, all are born imperfect and spend their lives trying to achieve a greater and greater degree of perfection. Some, of course, achieve it more closely than others, but he believed mankind should attempt to discover what the best conditions were for achieving perfection and then attempt to continually replicate it for the good of humanity.

This naturally led him to a question: just what kind of perfection can a person reach? He noticed that while animals are born into relatively similar circumstances and with similar skill sets, humans are not. They are instead incredibly adaptable to and dependent on their surroundings and their innate gifts, talents, drives, and desires. This degree of freedom allows for a wide range of abilities and achievements, but it also means that no one person can develop to perfection all the possibilities available to their species. Furthermore, whereas animals are mostly defined by their external circumstances, humanity has both internal and external forces to contend with. This means that while most animals are only at risk of being harmed by their environment, humans are at risk of not only that but also harming themselves or their community.

For example, power can be considered good. Should someone have the desire to attain power and influence to better the world around them, it could be helpful to the individual and their community. However, if power is only desired for power's sake, and a person makes it their sole mission to acquire more and more power, this will be detrimental to that person's growth as an individual and severely detrimental to their community as a whole. Similarly, in Aristotle's mind, human beings should not unduly devote themselves to one facet of life. Though when one is at work, relaxation seems appealing, the reality is that without work, these pleasures would become mere tedium.

Aristotle, as evidenced above, was a huge proponent of balance, believing that good and moral behavior could be found by striking a "golden mean" between excess and deficiency. As he notes in his work *Nicomachean Ethics:*

> [B]oth excessive and deficient exercise ruin bodily strength, and, similarly, too much or too little eating or drinking ruins health, whereas the proportionate amount produces, increases, and preserves it.

Much of his ideas and thought processes on ethics and philosophy were derived from empirical observation. Aristotle was known for collecting data and often exhorted his students to do the same. In one particular example, Aristotle urges his students to scrutinize the laws and political structures of all the known entities at the time to gather evidence on what they had done well and what had failed. In more recent times, Aristotle is mischaracterized as a dogmatic philosopher, but this is simply because his work is considered authoritative. If one looks at how Aristotle went about developing and expanding on his philosophy, it is quite clear that he is one of the foremost empirical philosophers in the world.

In 323 BCE, Aristotle's former student and ruler of the Macedonian Kingdom, Alexander the Great died at the shockingly young age of 32. With his passing, Athens, which had been under his control, grew antagonistic to Macedonian control. Aristotle fled north of the city due to the rising tensions and sadly died one year later in 322 BCE.

In the immediate aftermath of his death, his students, known as the Peripatetics, carried out similar work. Since Aristotle's interests and work were vast and diverse, this led to quite a proliferation of works in many different fields, though work in history was the most significant. His followers authored histories of philosophy, medicine, mathematics, astronomy, and civilization. The Peripatetics kept the Lyceum open, but it, unfortunately, did not have the staying power of Plato's Academy. While it continued to operate, it lost much of the influence it had enjoyed under Aristotle and paled in comparison to the authority that the Academy was afforded in Athens.

Aristotle's works were largely lost or abandoned for a couple of centuries. If the historian Strabo (63 BCE - 23 CE) is to be believed, his writings were left to molder in a basement somewhere in present-day Turkey, though these were likely not the only copies in existence. At some point during the first century CE, Aristotle's works were rediscovered and repopularized with many contemporary philosophers writing commentaries on his work. The gradual process of the Aristotelian Revival continued well into the Middle Ages and directly impacted the formation of philosophical thought throughout Europe.

Following Aristotle's death, political life in Greece took a turn. The city-states, which had already been ruled over by Alexander, lost even more power and influence until they gradually became political poker chips between the Hellenistic kings. Understandably, philosophical developments took a slightly different bent at this time, too. Rather than exploring deep questions about life, meaning, and existence or pondering political questions about how best to rule a nation, the newer philosophies were more interested in providing answers or comfort to their followers in a turbulent time.

The first of these schools, Stoicism, was developed by a merchant named Zeno of Citium (c. 335 - c. 263 BCE). After traveling to Athens on business, he began to listen to philosophical lectures, which eventually led to him developing his own way of thinking. He began to teach at the Stoa Poikile, a public hall, which is where Stoicism derives its name.

Zeno mostly combined the work of Socrates and Heraclitus, teaching that if a man wishes to be happy, he must live "in agreement" with himself. This was further refined over time, ultimately stating that one should "live in agreement with nature." For Zeno, the highest good a man can achieve is to be virtuous—not much else matters. Virtues come from acquiring knowledge of what the right choices are and having peerless self-control to go along with it. He also valued the virtues of fortitude, which he saw as knowledge of what is worth suffering for, and justice. For a Stoic, humanity's passions are the source of all the evils in the world and stem from a lack of self-control and an inability to clearly delineate what is good and what is not.

Similar to his black-and-white take on what was good and what was not, Zeno also initially stated that all men were either wise or fools. Later, and the reason why is unknown, he softened his stance slightly, allowing for a third option: men could be progressing towards wisdom.

Beyond just opinions on the individual actions of men, Zeno and his Stoics believed that the world was controlled by one divine entity known as *logos* (meaning "word" or "speech"). Likely inspired by Heraclitus' thoughts on logos, the Stoic logos sets the laws for the universe and keeps the world operating in an orderly fashion. It can never be disturbed by the actions of humanity, so when humans rebel against the laws set forth by the logos, they only bring harm to themselves.

Following Zeno's passing, the Stoic school was further fostered under Cleanthes (c. 331 - c. 232 BCE) and Chrysippus (c. 280 - c. 206 BCE). The latter is credited with forming a new kind of logic, propositional logic, which in present times is occasionally viewed as superior to Aristotle's conceptual logic. The philosophy spread beyond Greece to Rome at a time in which Rome was steadily growing in dominance and influence throughout the Western world. There, Panaetius of Rhodes (c. 180 - 109 BCE) adapted Stoic philosophy to make it more attractive to the wealthy upper classes of Rome. The ideas caught on, and Stoicism became a virtual religion to many in Rome as the Republic unraveled during a tumultuous civil war and slave uprising. It was particularly popular with those who sought to preserve the Republic against those with totalitarian aims, particularly the aims of one Julius Caesar. The most well-known Roman Stoic is Cato the Younger (95 - 46 BCE) who famously committed suicide after Caesar's victory.

Even as Rome morphed from a republic into an empire, Stoicism remained a guiding philosophy. The Stoic Seneca the Younger (c. 4 BCE - 65 CE) was an advisor to Emperor Nero and tasked with the dismal chore of keeping the morally dubious leader virtuous, he eventually failed and was forced to commit suicide by Nero himself.

The second school of thought that blossomed within the unstable political climes of Athens in the late 4th and early 3rd centuries BCE is Epicureanism. Often characterized as the polar opposite of Stoicism, this generalization, though fair, is not exactly accurate. Founded by Epicurus (341 - 270 BCE), he staunchly proclaimed, unlike Zeno, that the ideas behind the philosophy were his and his alone though portions, notably his explanation of the universe, were heavily influenced by Democritus' atomism.

While the Stoics offered virtue as the main source of human fulfillment, arguing that almost everything else bore no importance, Epicureans held that pleasure was the highest good. For Epicurus, seeking pleasure was the key to attaining a happy life. As was highlighted earlier in the text, the Stoics tended to seek out positions of power and influence, often wading into the political arena and becoming advisors to rulers and kings. Epicureans held no such ambitions, and Epicurus himself preferred to live amongst close followers and friends while tending to his garden. Furthermore, Stoics tended to gravitate toward the idea of "divine providence," which roughly means that whatever divine entity created the world has a plan and an active role in guiding creation. Epicureans, on the other hand, believed that the gods had little to no interest in the life and work of humanity.

From this description, it seems accurate then to characterize Stoicism and Epicureanism as polar opposites, but the two did have some foundational similarities. Even though Epicurus championed pleasure, it was not the kind of pleasure that runs in opposition to being morally good. Instead, he advocated seeking out life's little pleasures–this would make life tolerable and good even if circumstances like sickness, grief, or pain were encountered. Both Stoicism and Epicureanism were interested in providing a roadmap for their followers to look to during difficult times.

Epicureanism seemed to provide a way of life rather than just a philosophy for its followers. Although Epicurus had established a school known as Ho Kepos (The Garden) much like Plato's Academy and Aristotle's Lyceum, it was far more welcoming and laid back. Women were allowed to attend, and even famously, one of Epicurus' slaves named Mouse. Here, unlike the modern-day reputation of Epicureanism, nothing was taken to excess, with the most common drink at Ho Kepos being water. As Epicurus himself said, "Nothing is sufficient in life for the person who finds sufficiency too little."

Epicurus died at 72 from prostatitis, and according to all accounts, he passed gracefully illustrating his philosophy of serene, simple pleasures guiding him to the very end. Unfortunately, as the years passed and as the philosophy made its way over the Ionian Sea into Italy, Epicureanism became deeply misunderstood. During Roman times, to call oneself an Epicurean was to admit to living a dissolute, atheistic life defined by chasing as much pleasure as possible, to the point of utter debauchery.

A third philosophy, known as Skepticism, flourished right around the same time Stoicism was growing in popularity. Founded by Pyrrhon of Elis (c. 360 - c. 272 BCE), the philosophy does not seem to have possessed the same cultural cache as Stoicism and Epicureanism, but it is still historically relevant. Pyrrhon's philosophy asserts, much like Gorgias' sarcastic critique of philosophers written in the previous century, that no person can know anything for sure and what is observed by the senses cannot necessarily be trusted. However, the Skeptics are mostly remembered for one of Pyrrhon's students, Sextus Empiricus.

He wrote a verbose treatise called *Pros dogmatikous* (*Against the Dogmatists*), which was a critique of positivist philosophers. Positivists, unlike Skeptics, believe that knowledge can be attained through sensory experiences. It should be noted that Positivism was not officially articulated until the work of August Comte in the 19th century, but the underlying thought processes have been present in Western philosophy since the beginning. In his work, Sextus Empiricus quoted many great Greek philosophers, and it is through his work that many of the empiricists of 18th century Europe—like David Hume—studied ancient philosophy.

For the most part, philosophical development somewhat stalled during the Roman Empire. Instead of new schools of thought, the discussions were centered largely around remixing ideas that had originated with the Greeks. Stoicism, Epicureanism, and Skepticism remained popular, but slightly older belief systems, like ones that originated with Plato and Pythagoras, regained acclaim. These philosophical schools would remain in ascendency until the Byzantine Emperor Justinian I (483-565 CE) closed them down in 529 CE to further his Christian belief system.

Over time, certain aspects of the different popular philosophical schools of thought blended, so it was no longer purely Platonic or purely Pythagorean thought. Instead, Neoplatonism combined much of Plato's original ideas but also incorporated elements from Aristotle and the Stoic thinkers. Flourishing during the 3rd century CE, Neoplatonism was formed by Ammonius Saccas, a man who had been raised in the Christian faith but later abandoned it in favor of studying philosophy, particularly Plato. Much like Socrates, Ammonius never put pen to paper himself. What is known about Ammonius comes through a third party, namely the *Enneads*. These were a collection of writings from one of his disciples, Plotinus (205-270 CE). Oddly enough though, these writings were compiled not by Plotinus himself, but by his student Porphyry (234-305 CE). Therefore, much of what is referred to as Neoplatonism is distilled through two layers, and not directly from the source himself.

As mentioned earlier, Neoplatonism was a combination of multiple schools of thought, and it was also influenced by the religious and cultural tendencies of the time, particularly Christianity. Neoplatonists believed that there was a general hierarchy of Beings. At the top was the One or the Good, a divine entity that is indefinable in human language. Below the One resides nous, or intelligence, followed by souls. After souls comes the world that is readily discerned by the senses, and finally, at the base of the hierarchy is matter, the source of evil. In order for humans to achieve perfect happiness, they must be joined with the One. This unification can be accomplished through a combination of contemplation and purification. In Neoplatonic thought, it was possible to achieve this state of bliss multiple times–it was not a permanent place where one remained. Plotinus, it is said by Porphyry, has reached it seven times.

A further iteration of Neoplatonism was developed by Iamblichus of Chalcis (c. 250 - c. 330 CE). He folded neo-Pythagorean ideas into Neoplatonic thought, particularly the number theory that had so enamored Pythagoras. Iamblichus also expanded on the Neoplatonic hierarchy, incorporating the Greek pantheon of gods and goddesses.

However, pagan philosophy was fading. Christianity was gaining more and more social and political ground. This dwindling was accelerated once Justinian I ordered all the pagan schools to be closed in 529 CE, with only a branch of the Neoplatonic school remaining active in Alexandria, Egypt. The Athenian Neoplatonists fled even further east, finding a home at the Persian king Khosrow I's court. Six years later, the Neoplatonists were allowed to return to Athens, but the power of the pagan schools was gone. Christianity was now fully dominant, though as the Age of Antiquity gave way to the Middle Ages, the work and ideas of the Neoplatonists remained alive and influential within Christian theology and philosophy.

3

THE AGE OF CHRISTIAN ASCENDENCY - THE EARLY MIDDLE AGES (300S - 1200S CE)

After Plotinus, Greek theology lost its primacy, though this was likely due to the constrictions imposed by Justinian, and not some loss of ability on the part of Greek thinkers. Outside of Greece, the major power structure of the ancient world, Rome, was gradually crumbling. Though the fall of the Roman Empire is sometimes referred to as a singular event, it was, in fact, a slow, drawn-out process that lasted a painful two-and-a-half centuries. The period that followed was known as the Middle Ages. Lasting up to the Renaissance in the 15th century, medieval philosophy was largely dominated by Christian thought and theology, promulgated by churchmen instead of independent men.

However, medieval philosophy was more than repackaged Christian theology. Greek thought, particularly Neoplatonic ideals, was recast in a Christian light, as the church's early forefathers sought to supply a rational explanation for their faith. Neoplatonic philosophy was particularly useful since it already had a heavily mystical bent, thanks to Plotinus' exposure to Middle Eastern traditions. Later, Aristotle became more instrumental to medieval philosophers. On the whole, philosophy was used to prop up theology and faith throughout the Middle Ages, rather than being a wholly separate discipline. Though this intermarriage would not last, the period of Christian ascendency in Western philosophy left an indelible mark on European thought moving beyond the Renaissance.

The early Middle Ages, which dates from the fall of Rome to the 12th century, was a time of tumult and fear. Rome had been the dominant power in the region for centuries, and now with its dissolution, a massive power vacuum opened up. Various tribes scrapped for power throughout the continent, but over time, distinctive European cultures began to coalesce and emerge. The philosophers during these times were initially Romans and then later monks as European monasteries and churches grew in prominence.

St. Augustine of Hippo (354-430 CE), the first of these medieval thinkers, was born in the Roman province of Numidia in North Africa. Likely from a well-to-do family, he received an excellent education in rhetoric and philosophy. Though his mother, Monica, is characterized as a devout Christian and likely raised Augustine to have a passing familiarity with the faith, Augustine himself is said to have converted to Christianity around 386 CE when he was thirty-two years old after reading the New Testament treatise of Paul's letter to the Romans. Turning away from his former life, much to the delight of his pious mother, Augustine took a vow of celibacy and eventually was named the bishop of Hippo. The theological and philosophical doctrines he developed were foundational to Christianity and as a result, to Western thought as a whole.

If Paul was his awakening to Christian theology, it was the writings of Cicero that roused his initial interest in philosophy, though eventually he was more heavily influenced by the Neoplatonists. For Augustine, the Neoplatonist idea of a realm beyond the senses governed by the divine One dovetailed nicely with Christianity. He identified this eternal Truth as the Christian God from which all other eternal truths, like mathematics or ethics, flow. Knowledge and education were crucial for Augustine since he believed humanity cannot know God through their senses, but can rather seek him through their minds.

He took this separation of the world of the senses and the world of the divine even further, positing the separation of the body and the soul. Though that now is considered practically dogma among many people in Western nations, particularly Christians, Socrates, Plato, Aristotle, and now Augustine can be thanked for its proliferation. Augustine believed that human beings are made up of two substances: a body and a soul, and the soul, like the souls in the Neoplatonic hierarchy, is the superior of the two. The soul, according to Augustine, is immortal, because it is the portion of the human being that contains the eternal Truth of God.

Two other Augustinian philosophies were foundational: his concept of Original Sin and his just war theory. The former essentially claimed that because of the initial rejection of God in the Garden of Eden by Adam and Eve, each human was born in sin and damned to Hell. Baptism was necessary at birth to blot out this evil, but humanity is still prone to wicked and immoral behavior. As a result, humans could never achieve salvation and unity with God on their own merits, so grace from God in the form of the sacrifice of His Son, Jesus, is necessary for mankind to rejoin God in Heaven.

The latter, just war theory, is laid out in his work *The City of God*. It argues that there are cases where war is morally acceptable. He traces this reasoning back to Paul's letter to the Romans, which reminds the reader that God handed the power of the sword to human governments. Noting that "the purpose of all wars is peace," Augustine's ideas about the morality of war were further illustrated by later Christian thinkers like St. Anselm of Canterbury (1033-1109) and St. Thomas Aquinas (1225-1274), and echoes of it can even be found in the 20th century, embedded in the Geneva Convention's ideas about prisoners of war, treatment of civilians, and war crimes.

When Augustine died in 430, the Vandals were looming on the outskirts of Hippo. Rome as a political entity of any consequence effectively did not exist. As the lights of knowledge seemed to dim across the Western world, Boethius (c. 470 - 524) stood astride two eras, desperately preserving the work of his Greek and Roman forefathers for the European luminaries to come. Born into an aristocratic family in Rome, Boethius came of age at a time when the Ostrogoths were in control of the city. The city's wealthy classes continued to style themselves after their ancestors, dressing and behaving as they always had, but the Rome of their predecessors was slipping away from them. Boethius likely felt this quiet desperation and fear over a fading culture.

Concerned that the Roman upper classes were no longer being educated in the Greek language, Boethius began to translate the works of Aristotle and Plato into Latin. Unfortunately, his project was cut short when Theodoric, the king of the Ostrogoths, imprisoned, tortured, and put him to death. Though Boethius' life and work were truncated, it is through him that many of the medieval scholars who followed had access to the work and thought of Plato and Aristotle.

Aside from the efforts of Boethius, several Greek Fathers of the Church were instrumental in providing medieval Europe with access to ancient Greek philosophy. The most notable of these patristic writers were Origen (c. 185 - c. 254 CE), St. Gregory of Nyssa (c. 335 - 394), and St. Maximus the Confessor (c. 580 - 662). These theologians were heavily influenced by Neoplatonic thought, and when medieval intellectuals began to translate the work of the Greek Fathers, they were unwittingly bringing the work of the pagan Greek philosophers right along with them.

During the 9th century, one of the first Europeans to begin translating these texts was an Irishman named John Scotus Erigena (810 - c. 877 CE). Employed as a teacher of grammar and logic at the Carolingian court of King Charles II the Bald (823 - 877 CE), he worked to convert patristic literature from Greek into Latin.

He also wrote his own lengthy work, *On the Division of Nature*, which was essentially Christian theology arranged in Neoplatonic order. Much like Augustine before him, Erigena identified the Neoplatonic One as the Christian God from whom all beings originate. He also agreed with the Neoplatonic idea of eventual reunification with the One, arguing that through creation, all creatures come from God and will return to Him at the end of time.

The Carolingian dynasty that Erigena served controlled much of Europe throughout the 9th century. It was the initial iteration of the Holy Roman Empire founded by Charlemagne and it dominated European culture during the early Middle Ages. Its decline and collapse at the dawn of the 10th century coincided with a short period of intellectual paucity in Western Europe. Luckily, a political and cultural revival was not far off, and Otto I (912 - 973 CE), a German, managed to wrangle the empire back together in 963. This led to a cultural renaissance of sorts, and a new wave of Christian thinkers rose to the surface.

Benedictine monasteries, particularly those at Cluny and Gorze, were reinvigorated by reforms. There was a tendency among some in the consecrated life, like Peter Damian (1007 - 1072 CE), to look askance at secular philosophers. Damian and his compatriots feared that studying knowledge that wasn't from a religious source could lead to corruption and degradation of the faith. Luckily, not all involved in monastic life agreed, and as the early Middle Ages progressed, monasteries became bastions of learning and knowledge.

One such monk was, like Damian, also a member of the Benedictine Order. St. Anselm of Canterbury (1033 - 1109 CE), born in Italy and later named the Archbishop of Canterbury, is famous for his use of both faith and reason to find the truth. In the true Augustinian tradition, Anselm placed faith first but often used reason to justify it. When asked to author a meditation on God that proved his existence without the use of scriptures and through reason alone, he produced the *Monologian (Monologue)*. Written in 1077, it has three proofs for the existence of God, all of which borrow heavily from Neoplatonic philosophy. Essentially, Anselm acknowledges that there are many good and almost perfect things contained within the universe, but they can all be traced back to the sublimely perfect and supreme Good which is God.

Monologian was followed by *Proslogian (Allocution or Address)* roughly a year later. This work contains his most famous proof: an ontological argument for the existence of God. Simply put, Anselm posited that God is the greatest being in existence that humans can think of. Therefore, he must exist because no greater being than God can be conceived. Anselm's ontological argument differed from most attempts to prove God's existence in that there is no reliance on empiricism. Rather, Anselm argued that humanity can deduce that God exists simply by the definition of what God is.

However, the tension between those who feared secular philosophy and those who embraced it as a means to affirm their Christian faith continued. A Cistercian monk, St. Bernard de Clairvaux (1090 - 1153 CE), was one such doubter, leery of the influence of secularism on the faithful. He preferred mystical contemplation in lieu of scholarly pursuits, and his doctrine on mystical love remained significant to the Christian faith well beyond his lifetime.

On the other end of the spectrum was Peter Abelard (1079 - 1142 CE). Though Abelard eventually joined religious life, he began his philosophical career in the secular forum, founding several schools around Paris. As a celebrated logician, much of his methodology and work contributed to the Scholastic method, which will be discussed later. His seminal work *Sic et non* (*Yes and No*) presented both sides of prevalent theological arguments so that the proper answer could be fairly determined. Abelard's tendency to show both sides of an argument continued with the question of universals. In philosophy, universals refer to a certain quality that a person or thing must hold to be grouped with other similar persons or things. For example, for something to be considered a circle, it must have the universal quality of "roundness."

At the time, there were two opposing thoughts on universals. The first, the nominalists, believed that universals were only words, nothing more. The second, the realists, espoused a more Platonic worldview, arguing that a realm of universals separate from the human mind does indeed exist. Abelard straddled the line between these two, accepting and rejecting certain aspects of the nominalist and realist worldviews. He criticized the nominalists, asserting that names do indeed have meaning–they are not just arbitrary. As for the realists, he postulated that universals are a mental concept that refers to specific people or objects, but that the commonalities, like "humanity" being common to all human beings, come from God, who created all things from the same sacred thought.

Unfortunately for Abelard, his thoughts, particularly those on the Holy Trinity, ran counter to many accepted theological truths at the time, and he was frequently criticized, threatened, and censured by church leaders. He often found himself fleeing from cities, and even contemplated leaving the bounds of

Christendom entirely to preserve his life. After being condemned for heresy for the second time in 1140, Abelard withdrew from teaching and lived out his days as a monk in the monastery at Cluny.

Education, prior to the time of Abelard and his compatriots, had been largely focused on the medieval liberal arts of grammar, rhetoric, logic, geometry, arithmetic, music, and astronomy. There was also wide support for the reading of the Latin classics such as the *Odyssey*, the *Aeneid*, or the works of Herodotus. Gradually, trends in education changed to support a greater focus on logic and dialectics as well as added schooling on the scientific disciplines of the day, which included the study of philosophy. Within the field of philosophy, Plato's days of ascendency among medieval scholars were waning. Recent commentaries and translations of Aristotle from sources outside of Europe had been gaining popularity since before the late 12th century, much of Aristotle's work had been unknown to Europeans. As a result, educators were starting to favor Aristotle over Plato. This educational trend of focusing on the sciences and Aristotelian methods became known as Scholasticism.

The groundswell of information on Aristotle in Europe came from the Arabic world. Avicenna (980-1037 CE), as he was known in Europe (in Arabic, Ibn Sīnā), was a brilliant Persian thinker and leading luminary of the medieval Muslim world. Knowledgeable in a vast array of fields, particularly medicine, he is purported to be the author of as many as 240 texts. Avicenna was quite knowledgeable of Aristotle's ideas on metaphysics, and using this basis, wrote a metaphysical proof of God that was frequently dissected among Christian scholars. His works on psychology, rhetoric, and natural philosophy were also influential at the time and his encyclopedic work *Al-Qānūn fi al-ṭibb* (*The Canon of Medicine*) was considered the definitive text on medicine for several centuries.

Another Muslim thinker that was highly influential at this time was Averroës (1126 - 1198 CE) (in Arabic, Ibn Rushd). Hailing from the southern Spanish town of Córdoba, Averroës is credited for merging Islamic and Platonic thought. He was, however, not as well-liked among Christian circles. His philosophies were routinely attacked by medieval churchmen, who saw some of his doctrines as a threat to Christian theology. Being steeped in Platonic thought, Averroës promulgated the idea that at death, everyone is reunited with a single form like the Platonic One or the Abrahamic God. This was problematic for Christians who support the idea of individual immortality after death. Called "the Commentator" by medieval scholars, Averroës simply did not enjoy the same acceptance and widespread influence that Avicenna did due to his "anti-Christian" philosophies, but he remained impactful to the Scholastics.

Though the contributions of the Islamic scholars were far more crucial in forming Scholastic thought, there were also a handful of medieval Jewish scholars who played a role as well. Called Avicebron or Avicebrol by the Scholastics, Ibn Gabriol (c. 1022 - c. 1058) was a Spanish Jew from Málaga. At the time, he was believed to be either a Christian or a Muslim, and his most consequential work *Fons vitae* (*The Fountain of Life)* was originally written in Arabic. Historically, this makes sense since Gabriol was born while Málaga was under the control of the Caliphate of Córdoba and remained under Arabic control and influence for the duration of his life.

Scholastics enjoyed Gabriol's clear explanation of form and matter: all beings in existence have forms that classify what they are and they are composed of matter. This matter is either corporeal or spiritual, or in the case of human beings, both: a corporeal body and a spiritual soul. Gabriol also noted that one being can possess many forms or classifications. For example, a man is a living thing, an animal, and a human. It was a bit like rudimentary Linnaean taxonomy; introducing a kind of hierarchy of forms.

The second influential Jewish thinker, Moses Maimonides (1135 - 1204 CE), also known as Moses ben Maimon, or simply Rabbi Moses, attempted to reconcile the tension between faith and reason that had caused so much strife for the likes of Peter Abelard. His work, the *Dalālat al-hā'irīn (The Guide for the Perplexed)*, argued that there was no need for a contradiction between reason and faith since both were given to man by the Divine. Any opposition that arises between the two is due to the failure of man, either in translating the word of God or in devising various philosophies. He also punched holes in the Aristotelian argument for an infinite universe. Essentially, if God is omnipotent and all-powerful, then He can decide the bounds of the universe, making it finite or infinite.

With this sudden influx of Greek, Islamic, and Jewish thought, as well as their own Christian and European intellectual developments, Europe entered into a kind of academic explosion. Scholastic thinkers began to establish schools of higher learning, most notably in France, Paris to be specific, and Oxford in England.

It should be noted that although the Scholastics are lumped together, this is mostly by virtue of their place in history. Though there was somewhat universal respect for certain philosophical voices like the Fathers of the Church (one of whom is the aforementioned

Augustine), Plato, Aristotle, and Avicenna, and most Scholastic educators taught through the methods of a lecture followed by a formal debate. There is no one unifying thought that epitomizes Scholasticism, and most scholars were left to their own devices to develop their philosophies. Rather, Scholasticism is marked by a common time as well as certain influences and qualities, rather than one central, shared philosophy.

So, who were these Scholastics - these Schoolmen? Many of them, as in the generation before, were churchmen, dedicated to the integration of faith and reason. Roger Grosseteste (c. 1175 - 1253) was an English bishop and the first chancellor of the University of Oxford. He gave the medieval Western world its first copy of Aristotle's *Nicomachean Ethics* which he translated from Greek to Latin and he authored several commentaries on Aristotle's other works. A scientifically-minded individual, Grosseteste became increasingly captivated by the study of optics which looks at the behavior of light through a scientific and mathematical lens. His interest in light led him to a philosophical idea that he outlined in his book *De luce (On Light)*, postulating that light is the basic component that all things are built from, and God is the one eternal light of the world.

His student, Roger Bacon (c. 1220 - 1292), building off of his mentor's love for science and the Scientific Method, heavily supported experimentation to reach scientific conclusions, popularizing the term "experimental science" through his writing. Much like Augustine, Bacon supported the idea of dual enlightenment through exploration of the world via the senses and divine inspiration from God in the mind. His driving goal was to identify a kind of "universal wisdom" that operated on theological rules and could contain all the varying disciplines of science. He also had hoped for all of Christendom to join together and create one society led by the pope.

Across the Channel at the University of Paris, William of Auvergne (c. 1180 - 1249), who later became the bishop of Paris, remained skeptical of the "new" philosophies trickling in from the Arab world. He was resistant to the ideas of Aristotle and Avicenna, claiming that pagan and Islamic thought threatened the sanctity of the Christian faith. He also inadvertently agreed with the Jewish thinker, Moses Maimonides, when it came to Aristotle's theory of an eternal world. He, like Maimonides, believed that Aristotle was mistaken in positing that the world was infinite, but unlike Maimonides, Auvergne said this particular Aristotelian doctrine ran counter to the Christian idea of creation.

Continuing his defense of creation through a Christian lens, Auvergne also heartily disagreed with Avicenna's concept of creation. Avicenna believed the universe had been created through a kind of divine meditation, and this act of creation was something that had to be done. Christians, Auvergne among them, believe that creation is an action that was freely and willingly taken by God. There was no absolute reason for creation–humanity being a central part of that–to exist outside of God's desire for it to come into being. This ties mankind–and all of creation–inextricably to God and God's will.

Much like William of Auvergne, St. Bonaventure (1217-1274 CE), a Franciscan friar from Italy studying at the University of Paris, looked askance at the Arabic and pagan philosophies. He believed Aristotle to be intelligent and talented, particularly honoring his work in the natural sciences, but when it came to philosophical thought, Bonaventure overwhelmingly preferred the ideas of Plato and Plotinus to those posited by Aristotle. Bonaventure thought that philosophy desperately needed faith to guide the discipline, and since Aristotle was a pagan who denied the existence of the divine, his thought processes were inherently flawed.

By ignoring God's supreme role in both creation and future power over the world, Bonaventure found Aristotle's philosophies guilty of a "three-fold blindness."

These three problems were Aristotle's idea of an eternal world, his concept of all mankind sharing one intellect, and his belief that there is no punishment or reward following the death of the body. It would be easy to say then that Bonaventure eschewed all pagan philosophy, but as mentioned earlier, he was partial to the works of Plato and Plotinus. Bonaventure acknowledged that their status as pagans made the full truth of the world unattainable to them, but appreciated how close they came to it in his mind. For Bonaventure, philosophy was a part of the human journey to God; not completely enmeshed in theology, but not a completely separate discipline either.

Deeply influenced by Augustinian thought, Bonaventure's philosophical journey to God was inspired by the idea that all human souls are stamped by God–made in his image and likeness. As a result, all humans are built with a drive to seek the Creator, and this is done through the acquisition of knowledge and divine revelation. Thus, with this in mind, Bonaventure was able to reformulate Anselm's ontological argument for God. All humans are born with the idea of God in their hearts and minds–why else would that be if not for God? His incisive ontological statement was "Si Deus est Deus, Deus est," or "If God is God, God is."

However, not all of the European continental philosophers cast such a wary eye on the incoming philosophical influences. A German-born Dominican bishop, St. Albertus Magnus (c. 1200 - 1280 CE) or more simply, St. Albert the Great, was quite excited by the potential value held by both the Greek philosophers of antiquity and the newer Arabic scholars. Unlike Auvergne and Bonaventure, Albert was quite drawn to Aristotle, considering him the greatest philosopher. He strove to educate his contemporaries on Aristotelian thought, and the ascendency of Aristotle throughout the Middle Ages can largely be attributed to his work and the work of his student, St. Thomas Aquinas (c. 1224 - 1274).

Albert, though also honored for his vital contributions to the natural sciences, was also quite consequential in the field of philosophy. He realized that, for a Christian world, some of Aristotle's philosophical teachings would seem to be lacking, and he worked to fill in the gaps that he observed. Though his student, Aquinas, did the more philosophical heavy lifting, Albert should still be credited for smoothly synthesizing Aristotelian and Neoplatonic thought with Christian philosophy, utilizing the teachings of early Christian thinkers like Augustine alongside non-Christians Aristotle, Avicenna, and Ibn Gabriol.

While Albert had managed to blend many different schools of thought, it was Aquinas who managed to make them all extremely popular and palatable to European Christians. Aquinas, another Dominican priest, was like his mentor, passionate about the interplay of faith and reason. Perhaps inspired by the teachings of Moses Maimonides, Aquinas echoed his beliefs that faith and reason are inherently non-contradictory since they are both gifts from God to humanity. He was also, like Albert, quite enamored with Aristotle, and blamed Christian Europeans' skepticism of the ancient philosopher on the commentaries provided by the Arabic thinkers like Avicenna and Averroës. To mitigate this, Aquinas embarked on his own Aristotelian commentaries, eager to show his peers that Aristotle's system could be seamlessly integrated into Christian thought.

To accomplish this, he heavily borrowed from Aristotle's philosophy, but painted it with a decidedly Christian brush. For example, the "unmoved mover" discussed by Aristotle became the Judeo-Christian God and Aquinas agreed with Aristotle's assertion that the soul is a person's form, while the body is the matter. However, Aquinas disagreed with Aristotle's idea that the soul was not immortal or that it encoded the inherent value of a person, as those two ideas would clash with Christian doctrine. Aquinas adapted Aristotelian philosophy to fit Christianity, not the other way around. Whenever he encountered something that conflicted with the faith, he simply reshaped the ancient Greek ideas to match medieval Christian temperament. He aimed to demonstrate to his students and readers that this new agreement he was demonstrating between Christian philosophy and Greco-Arabic thought was simply a result of a new understanding of old ideas.

His works *Summa Theologiae* (sometimes referred to as the *Summa Theologica* or just the *Summa*) and *Summa contra gentiles* (*Summa Against the Gentiles*) became guiding lights for Christian philosophy moving into the later Middle Ages, and continue to be influential on Catholic thought and doctrine into the present day. However, instead of continuing to force deeper intermarriage of theological and philosophical thought, these works clearly laid out the distinctions between the two. Philosophers should look to data compiled by the senses while theologians should rely on Sacred Scripture. To Aquinas, a philosopher's role was to question everything, but a theologian's role was to appeal to the authority of God's Word. This small crack that Aquinas identified between philosophers and theologians would continue to deepen and widen into a chasm as the centuries passed.

Aside from Aquinas' assertions on the difference between theologians and philosophers, most scholars in the early Middle Ages tended to be vehemently Christian, and their philosophies and methodologies of teaching reflected that. There was, however, an exception in the Averroists in Paris. Like Albert the Great and Aquinas, the Averroists welcomed Aristotle's ideas with open arms, but unlike the two aforementioned saints, the Averroists taught and promulgated Aristotelian philosophy even when it contradicted Christian ideals. The Averroists are called such because though they taught Aristotelian philosophy, they mostly looked to Averroës' commentaries on Aristotle for guidance. The term "Latin Averroists" is also used to describe this group since they chiefly taught in the Latin language.

Led by Siger de Brabant (1240 - c. 1281), these men wanted to be philosophers only and believed that humanity should follow reason to its natural conclusion, even if that contradicts the faith of the day. Two doctrines the Averroists supported that Christian thinkers found particularly offensive were the Aristotelian ideas of the eternal universe and the singular intellect shared by all humanity. Yet, many of these scholars retained their Christian faith, and so were frequently attacked for holding a "double truth;" that is, holding two contradictory ideas to be true in one's mind.

The rise of the Averroists heralded a decisive slant toward rationalism and seemed to vindicate Christian scholars' fears that the intrusion of Greco-Arabic thought on Christian society would lead to a fragmentation of faith. The Church, which at this time was the unified Catholic Church under the pope in Rome, attacked the perceived threat accordingly. Giles of Rome (c. 1243 - 1316) authored a scathing treatise in 1270, *Errores philosophorum (Errors of the Philosophers)*, while the bishops in Paris and Canterbury released condemnations of various philosophical ideas, including some penned by Aquinas. The commingling of religion and philosophy wasn't necessarily over as the thirteenth and fourteenth centuries unfolded, but there was an emphatic split between the two that would only grow as time passed.

4

A PIVOT IN THE LATE MIDDLE AGES (1250 CE - 1500 CE)

Moving into the Late Middle Ages, an era coded by historians as existing from around 1250 to 1500 CE, much of the philosophical thought initiated in the Early Middle Ages continued and was solidified. After the passing of Siger de Brabant, Averroism was continued by John of Jandun (c. 1286 - 1328), and though it did not enjoy any kind of increased support or popularity, it remained an active philosophical faction into the early days of the Renaissance.

On the more religious side of things, Aquinas enjoyed quite a bit of posthumous fame with his philosophy, dubbed Thomism, becoming the official mode of teaching for the Dominican order. In the Catholic religious traditions, Dominican priests and nuns are among those most dedicated to education and the pursuit of *veritas*, or truth. Dominican brothers and sisters often carry the moniker of O.P. after their names, meaning Order of Preachers. Dominicans treat education as a form of preaching through which to live out their religious vows. As a result, Thomism was the philosophy through which many young people were educated during this time and it continues to play a role in Catholic education today.

However, a different religious order, the Franciscans, began to develop their own philosophical leanings that directly competed with Thomism at this time. Two members of the order, John Duns Scotus (c. 1265 - 1308 CE) and William of Ockham (c. 1285 - c. 1348 CE), were particularly consequential.

Also known as Doctor Subtilis (the Subtle Doctor), John Duns Scotus, or John Duns the Scot, was–as his name suggests–a Scottish priest in the Franciscan Order. While there was a growing idea among rationalist philosophers that philosophy alone was enough to satiate the human desire to seek the truth, Duns Scotus greatly opposed this notion. Believing that mankind was instead made with a dual thirst for both knowledge and God, Duns Scotus argued that pre-Christian philosophers, Aristotle chief among them, could not have possibly been able to fully comprehend human nature. He noted that man seeks knowledge through the senses alone due to their fallen nature, that is, the condition of mankind after being exiled from the biblical Garden of Eden. Thus, Aristotle was wrong to suppose this is the only way to gain knowledge. Rather, this limitation to the senses is simply a condition of sin and not the way God intended humanity to be. He, like St. Bonaventure, tended to favor a more Anselmian way of thinking about God, rather than the Aristotelian/Thomist way. God is an infinite being, not a primary mover. Scotus' proof of the existence of God is frequently considered not only one of the most complicated, but also the most impressive.

Similar to William of Auvergne's repudiation of Avicenna, Duns Scotus argued that the universe and all its inhabitants were created by God because he wanted to; the world was not, in his mind, the result of some inevitable act, but rather an act of God's loving free will. Contrasting Aquinas who championed the primacy of the intellect, Duns Scotus argued instead that will is supreme over intellect. For medieval scholars, an example would be the belief that morality stems from God's will rather than from his intellect or knowledge. This school of thought, known as voluntarism, continued to grow and morph in varying directions, ultimately influencing the likes of modern luminaries like Nietzsche and Freud.

Duns Scotus also revisited the Platonic idea of universals—last mentioned in this text with Peter Abelard. For him, universals refer to abstract concepts, not an actual realm as Plato had posited. This nuanced approach to universals earned him his nickname, "Doctor Subtilis." The abstract concepts he discussed were often commonalities shared by certain groups that are difficult to fully quantify or define, like the concept of humanity. However, Duns Scotus also allowed for individuality (*haecceitas*) that is not shared. For example, all humans have a shared humanity, but each human has a *haecceitas* (or individuality) that makes them who they are. The universal of humanity is repeatable ad nauseam, but the *haecceitas* is not. It is specific to each individual.

Though Duns Scotus and William of Ockham were not that far away from one another, historically speaking, Ockham's work and the philosophies of those that followed were, by the tail end of the 14th century, referred to as "the modern way," while Scotism and its contrasting Thomism were referred to as "the old way." William of Ockham was another Franciscan hailing from the isle of Britain, though his hometown near Surrey in England lay a bit further south than Duns Scotus' native Scotland.

Like Duns Scotus, Ockham was interested in defending the Christian faith against what he saw as intrusions from pagan and Islamic philosophies. He too supported the idea of creation out of God's free will rather than out of necessity. However, unlike Duns Scotus, he largely rejected the idea of universals, embracing a form of nominalism. Basically, Ockham adhered to the idea that God creates everything uniquely, without any kind of form or template. Naturally, some of these things have similarities that humans then use to name and categorize them, but there is little more to that than a name—hence the term "nominalism."

Because of his belief that God could essentially create the universe in any manner he wanted, Ockham suggested that the laws of the universe and, in conjunction, the laws of morality, only are the way they are because God willed them so. He notes that—in Christian terms—it is considered morally good to love God only because that is how He wishes it to be. God could have made it so that it is instead considered morally good to hate Him or to feel neutral toward Him.

Ockham was also not inclined to trust that humans could grasp truth through reasoning alone, believing that philosophers must be satisfied with arguments of probability instead. Another tendency espoused by Ockham was to favor simpler explanations over more complex ones when searching for an answer, or "entities should not be multiplied beyond necessity." Though this was not a thought process unique to Ockham, he used it so frequently that it became known as "Ockham's razor" (also spelled "Occam").

Unfortunately, Ockham's ideas were not welcomed by all. Accused of teaching heresy in 1324, he was summoned to Avignon by Pope John XXII. Avignon, at the time, was the papal seat due to conflicts with the French crown. Two years later, his teachings were pilloried by a papal commission, but he was never officially charged with heresy. Ultimately, in 1328, at the behest of a Franciscan leader named Michael de Cesena, Ockham reviewed the writings of Pope John XXII and accused the pope himself of heresy. He was officially excommunicated that same year by the Catholic Church after fleeing Avignon. He resided first in Pisa and later settled in Munich where he died somewhere between 1347 and 1349. His teachings, known as Ockhamism, though controversial and even outlawed in Paris by 1474, remained well-liked and held the same importance as Thomism and Scotism. Ockham represented a fundamental shift to a more skeptical worldview that was embraced by many.

His work, especially his distrust of the abilities of human reason, inspired the likes of Nicholas of Autrecourt (c. 1300 - c. 1350 CE). Autrecourt argued that Aristotelianism was fundamentally antithetical to Christian belief and believed philosophy would be better off returning to the atomistic explanation of the world developed by Democritus and other ancient Greeks.

It seemed that just as quickly as Aristotelian philosophy gained its ascendancy through the likes of St. Albert the Great and St. Thomas Aquinas, it was already on the decline. Though it remained intact at universities and other institutions of education, Aristotelian thought began a steady decline that continued into the Renaissance. Platonic and Neoplatonic ideas were coming back into vogue and would continue to grow.

One such proponent of Neoplatonic thought was the Dominican Johannes Eckhart (c. 1260 - c. 1327 CE) or Meister (Master) Eckhart. Born in Thuringia, which is today in southeastern Germany, Eckhart was one of the foremost mystics of his time, and directly responsible for the proliferation of mystical thought in Germany during the Middle Ages. Christian mystics are often transfixed by the idea of having a transcendent encounter and union with the Divine. Some practices of mysticism can be as simple as contemplation of the Holy Scripture and as obscure as divine visions and mystical union with the Creator.

Mysticism for Eckhart involved a mixture of his Christian faith with Neoplatonic thought, particularly the idea that the soul can reach and unite with God through a combination of purification and knowledge. His ideas echoed those of Erigena in the 800s, particularly that God is the highest being, the Neoplatonic "One." However, Eckhart was quite clear that this status of "being" did not give creation parity with God, since creation is also made up of "beings." Rather, all other beings exist only because of God's gift of life.

Eckhart, though popular, ran afoul with the pope, as many intellectuals were wont to do at the time. He was called to Avignon and charged with heresy, to which he replied, "I may err but I am not a heretic, for the first has to do with the mind and the second with the will!" Much of Eckhart's philosophy, though possessing roots in Christian thought, Greco-Arabic ideas, and Neoplatonism, was still largely based on his own personal mystical experiences with God.

Like Eckhart, Nicholas of Cusa (1401 - 1464 CE) eschewed Aristotelian thought in favor of Neoplatonism. A German-born priest, Cusa, like many before him, took issue with Aristotle's claim of an infinite universe. To him, only God was capable of absolute infinity. That being said, the universe, as a reflection of God, can be said to possess relative infinity. He posited that there was no center of the universe and no stillness in the universe, rather, everything is relative to where in the universe the observer is located. This is a somewhat sophisticated explanation and has commonalities with modern scientific and philosophical thoughts on the universe.

Duns Scotus, Ockham, Eckhart, and Cusa, though not always supported by the religious leaders of the era, had initiated a philosophical shift through their preference for Plato over Aristotle. Though, as mentioned earlier, the philosophies of Aristotle continued to be taught, it was the philosophies of Plato and the Neoplatonists that enjoyed more acclaim and nuanced interpretations as the dawn of the Renaissance approached.

I truly hope that you're enjoying *A Brief History of Western Philosophy*. If you have feedback, whether positive or negative, please leave a review. My goal is to provide the best possible books for you, and your reviews are crucial in achieving that.

5

POLITICS, MEN, AND NATURE - THE RENAISSANCE (1400S - 1600S CE)

Any philosophy naturally reflects the world from which it arises. In the Middle Ages, the Catholic Church was the preeminent power in the Western world, and the political order was fractured among kings and nobles, ruling the masses through Feudalism. It is no surprise then that the philosophers of that time were also theologians and Churchmen, concerned mainly with questions of religious importance and preoccupied with how philosophy would impact faith. Access to education was typically through a religious organization in some way, and as a result, only an elite, ecclesiastical class was able to make their mark on philosophy.

Yet, this would not be the case forever. Three new technological developments arrived in Europe from the

East during the Middle Ages, and their advent marked a decisive turn in society. These three advancements were gunpowder, the printing press, and the compass. Gunpowder, which arrived from China during the 13th century, made the old political order of Feudalism much less secure. Previously, the feudal lord's thick castle walls were somewhat impenetrable, making him and his estate a necessary component for survival during conflicts. Gunpowder made the destruction of those walls much easier, and the necessity of a feudal system slowly faded.

Movable type, which is necessary for the printing press to work, had been in use since the 1000s or so in China. However, sometime around 1450, German-born Johannes Gutenberg developed the mechanical printing press, which greatly improved the availability of information. Books and learning were no longer the purviews of the ecclesiastical class alone, and an explosion of information followed.

Finally, the compass, which had been in use in China as far back as the Han Dynasty (206 BCE - 220 CE), greatly changed the scope with which mariners could navigate. Though some theorize that Europeans eventually developed the compass on their own, it is more likely that the technology passed from the Chinese to the Arabic world, and then arrived in Europe. Having previously used celestial guidance, the addition of a compass made it possible for them to travel ever greater distances. This led directly to the European arrival in the Western Hemisphere.

These three innovations changed the landscape of society. The Church was no longer the highest political and academic power. The Reformation that began with Martin Luther (1483 - 1546 CE) in 1517 fractured the religious dominance of the Catholic Church and her pope, while the increasing use of vernacular languages in writing made possible by the printing press decimated the supremacy of the Church's language, Latin. On the whole, the world grew increasingly preoccupied with the secular over the divine, as kings, nations, and empires grew greatly in strength and influence. Philosophers, rather than identifying themselves by their religious order or position on the clerical hierarchy, instead became concerned with their national identity.

Essentially, the Renaissance, which is typically noted as lasting from around 1400 to around 1600, was a time of rebellion; in philosophy, this was directed against the Church and her authority, the work of Aristotle, and Scholasticism. Instead of focusing on these three things, philosophers in the Renaissance focused on political philosophy, humanity, and nature.

Politics had been a chief concern of philosophy before the Middle Ages, and now with the feudal system crumbling and nations coalescing, it seemed prepared to take center stage again. Particularly in France, Italy, England, and Holland, philosophers tackled questions dealing with the morality of power, the needs of the state, and the needs of the people.

The most renowned of all political philosophers in this time period–and still considered renowned today–was Niccolò Machiavelli (1469 - 1527 CE). Unlike the previous luminaries discussed in the last chapter, Machiavelli was a statesman, living a completely secular life. Ultimately derided as an atheist and a misanthrope with poor morals thanks to the ideas laid out in his most well-known work, *Il Principe (The Prince)*, Machiavelli came from a wealthy Florentine family. He rose in political prestige quite quickly, becoming the head of the second chancery in Florence with no prior experience at the age of 29. This position placed the young Machiavelli in charge of all of Florence's foreign affairs and put him in proximity to the Italian political juggernauts of the day, like members of the Borgia family. One of the sons of the family, Cesare (1475 - 1507 CE), the illegitimate son of Pope Alexander VI (1431 - 1503 CE), was of particular interest to Machiavelli and became the inspiration behind *The Prince*.

Though the prominent Medici family ruled Florence from 1434 to 1737, there was a brief interlude from 1494 to 1512 when they were not in power. This happened to be the time Machiavelli was appointed to the second chancery, and when the Medici family returned to Florence in 1512, Machiavelli was suspected of conspiracy and exiled. While living outside the city, he wrote *The Prince* and dedicated it to Lorenzo de' Medici (1492 - 1519 CE). The work was essentially advice from Machiavelli to de' Medici on how to stay in power based on his observations of Cesare Borgia. While he earned the Medici family's good graces, when the family lost control of the city again for a brief period beginning in 1527, Machiavelli was not welcomed by the interim government. He died that same year.

However, his ideas lived on long after his passing. In *The Prince*, his notions about power–both how to seize it and how to keep it–sacrificed accepted morality for the needs of the state. Furthermore, that text and another of his works, *Discourses on the First Ten Books on Livy* served as the blueprint for diplomacy during the Renaissance era. Though he had a reputation for immorality, the truth was that Machiavelli hoped a return to the Roman virtues of antiquity would unite all the various Italian city-states into one nation of Italy. Machiavelli's notorious reputation may or may not be deserved, but there is no denying the impact he had on modern political philosophy. He championed nationalism and the exemption of the state from the accepted laws of morality, and these are two ideas that are still rampant in the 21st century.

Much like Machiavelli, Thomas Hobbes (1588 - 1679 CE) was another political philosopher who took a somewhat dim view of humanity and its natural proclivities. Born in Westport, a small village in the English county of Wiltshire, Hobbes was the son of a vicar with a violent temper. Abandoned by his father at age four, he was raised by his uncle and managed to ingratiate himself with the upper classes of England through his employment with the wealthy Cavendish family.

Hobbes believed that the natural state of life for humans was "solitary, poor, nasty, brutish, and short," and that men are naturally aggressive and inclined to war and chaos over peace and prosperity. Each person is interested only in their personal gain, and the purpose of government is, essentially, to protect men from one another. This directly contradicts the political philosophy of Aristotle, who thought that men reached their highest potential by becoming a citizen and living amongst one another in a *polis* (city).

Democracy, or any form of self-government, was ridiculous to Hobbes, who believed that men's natural belligerence would be the ruin of all. Instead, it would be better to agree to a social contract that sacrificed personal liberty for security. That is, submitting to a sovereign lord, most likely a king, and forfeiting private rights and property in exchange for safety and protection. This ruler is then allowed to make all the decisions for his people: who owns what, what the laws will be, and so on. The only way a ruler should be removed from this position is if he proves himself too weak to protect his people and his nation. Then, his subjects are no longer obligated to obey him since they are not receiving the safety they were guaranteed in exchange for their freedom.

To Hobbes, the power of the state should be absolute, even when it came to matters of faith. Believers, in his mind, should have no issues following what their sovereign demanded of them. This was a departure from previous political and philosophical thought, which placed the Catholic Church and her officers higher than the kings of the day. Hobbes was not simply advocating for a separation of church and state, but for a subordination of the church to the state.

Active during the tumultuous years before, during, and after the English Civil War (1642 - 1651 CE), Hobbes fled England for Paris, where he authored his works *De Cive, De Corpore,* and most notably of all, *Leviathan.* Both *De Cive* and *Leviathan* discuss the political philosophies that have been examined above, and the intended audience for both works, but particularly *Leviathan* was certainly meant to be the ruling class. Hobbes even gave a special copy to his pupil in Paris– the young Prince Charles who would later become King Charles II of England. Though Hobbes also contributed significantly to the field of natural science, optics, particularly, his most enduring contribution is his idea of the social contract. This greatly influenced the thinkers of the Enlightenment who succeeded him, particularly John Locke (1632 - 1704 CE), Immanuel Kant (1724 - 1804 CE), and Jean-Jacques Rousseau (1712 - 1778 CE).

Political philosophy during the Renaissance was definitively supportive of absolutism, which is no surprise considering the reigning kings of the day, principally the Stuart line in England and the Bourbon line in France, were vehement absolutists. As the Bourbon King Louis XIV said, "L'etat, c'est moi" (I am the state). However, despite their lengthy treatises on power and politics, Renaissance philosophers could never quite get away from the moral philosophy given to the West by Socrates. The ideas of human virtue and the moral laws of nature seemed to haunt even Machiavelli, and as a result, political theory and philosophy through the Renaissance and into the early modern period walked a fine line between political brawn and moral righteousness.

This secularization of philosophy continued beyond just the political theorizers. Education at this time resurrected fields of study that had been largely ignored during the Middle Ages, including mathematics, medicine, and Greek and Roman literature. The renewed interest in mathematics and medicine helped to fuel the Scientific Revolution, while the focus on classical literature spawned the humanist movement. These humanists emphasized the centrality of human beings rather than concerning themselves with the mysteries of the Divine.

Inspired by Plato, many humanist philosophers ignored the rhetoric advocated by Aristotelian Scholasticism in the Middle Ages in favor of the Platonic dialogue. Writers of the age began to use this framework again as opposed to the great treatises of the Middle Ages, typified by Aquinas' *Summa*. Even one of Machiavelli's works, *The Art of War*, is framed as a dialogue taking place in a Florentine garden.

This reborn love of Plato was especially potent in Medici-controlled Florence, where Marsilio Ficino (1433 - 1499 CE) translated all of Plato's available works into Latin. Ficino fostered a group of scholars in the city, known as the Platonic Academy. The members fancied themselves to be the newest iteration of the Academy founded by Plato in ancient Greece. One of the members, Giovanni Pico della Mirandola (1463 - 1494 CE), produced one of the defining humanist texts: *Oration on the Dignity of Man*.

However, the most profound impact that Plato had on Renaissance humanists was in their morality. Platonic morals were the accepted norm of the age, seen as the roadmap for the perfect courtier and gentlemen, and the virtues of wisdom, courage, and moderation were especially lauded. Humanism had a broader reach in Renaissance society and was much more than just a philosophical school of thought. It was a moral and literary idea as well–a general way of thinking that characterized a Renaissance man. Thinkers like renowned theologian Desiderius Erasmus (1466 - 1536 CE), St. Thomas More (1478 - 1535 CE) (the unlucky advisor to English King Henry VIII) and French writer Michel de Montaigne (1532 - 1592 CE) were all touched by humanist ideas and their writings and reputations clearly reflected this.

It should be remembered that the rediscovery of Plato also meant the rediscovery of other notable Greek philosophies like Pythagoreanism, atomism, Stoicism,

Skepticism, and Epicureanism. Pythagoreanism was especially valuable to the fields of mathematics and science. The work of Nicolaus Copernicus (1473 - 1543 CE), Galileo Galilei (1564 - 1642 CE), and Johannes Kepler (1571 - 1630 CE) in the area of astronomy and planetary motion can be directly attributed to Pythagorean influence.

When *Outlines of Pyrrhonism* authored by one of the famed skeptics, Sextus Empiricus, was found and translated in 1562, French philosophy was gripped by a wave of skepticism that influenced thinkers for the better part of a century from Montaigne to Descartes. Additionally, the rediscovery of the works of Epictetus and Seneca revived Stoicism in the Renaissance, with many looking to that particular school of thought for ethical guidance.

Philosophers in the Renaissance, as in earlier periods, were often not philosophers in the way modernity defines them. Philosophy was not a narrow discipline, and it is common when looking back into history that the great philosophers were also interested and proficient in other disciplines like science or math. Pythagoras and Plato were philosophers and mathematicians. Aristotle was a scientist. The field of physics was referred to as "natural philosophy" until the passing of Sir Isaac Newton in 1727. Thus, it is no surprise that the Renaissance focus on the natural world in philosophy involved a great many individuals who might traditionally be cast as scientists.

With the rediscovery of the Greek and Latin classics, as well as the renewed interest in science and mathematics, Renaissance philosophers looked at the world in a different light than their Scholastic counterparts had in the Middle Ages. The Schoolmen had been largely interested in the hierarchy of the universe as well as the influence and role of God. Renaissance thinkers were more interested in the physical works of the universe: what forces were at play, what data could be gathered, and how mathematics could explain them both.

This new supremacy of empiricism, scientific thought, and mathematical explanation served as the foundation for modern science and philosophy. Nature, it seemed, was explainable through math and science, and not so mysterious after all. This can be exemplified in the work of Andreas Vesalius (1514 - 1564 CE), a doctor from Belgium. His work would not have been possible during earlier centuries, but with the explosion of curiosity and thirst for learning in the Renaissance, he was the right man at the right time in history.

Known as the founder of human anatomy, he performed dissections on human cadavers, which was not unheard of, but still frowned upon at the time. He made massive strides in the field of medicine, able to empirically observe and discuss the vascular, muscular, and neural systems in the body. Though Vesalius made some mistakes–particularly when it came to female reproductive anatomy–his medical contributions argued a solid case for empirical experimentation and observation.

Like Vesalius, Galileo's work was perfectly timed with this moment in history, though he tended to favor mathematical explanations over observational ones. The use of Greek mathematics and the employment of new technologies like the telescope paired with this Renaissance-era certainty that the universe could be eventually explained through math. Though, unlike Vesilius' internal work, Galileo's work focused on the external, mostly the movement of the celestial bodies. He is often heralded as a hero of modern science, and he was truly an intellectual giant, developing the Galilean telescope, a rudimentary microscope, and a precursor to the thermometer. He was the first to observe many celestial happenings, including the mountains on the moon, the phases of Venus, and the rings of Saturn. His work, and the work of many other philosophers of the Renaissance era, clearly laid the groundwork for the Scientific Revolution and the many philosophies that would spawn in the modern world.

The Renaissance was an interesting, hybrid time. Caught between the religious dogmatism of the Middle Ages and the scientific explosion of the modern age, it was, for all of its fame, a transitional era for the West. By the end, the Catholic Church was no longer the arbiter of political power, and kings saw themselves on equal ground with the pope in Rome. Education was no longer relegated to the religious classes, and the answers to life's questions seemed to lay no longer with religion, but with science.

6

THE PHILOSOPHER-SCIENTIST: THE SCIENTIFIC REVOLUTION AND THE AGE OF ENLIGHTENMENT (1543 - 1815 CE)

Although history is split into neat blocks for students to easily digest, the reality is not so clear-cut. One era slowly bleeds into another, with the ideas morphing and commingling. It is only with the luxury of distance and time that one can see clear themes that accompany various eras, though these are hardly relegated to the tidy chunks of time inscribed in the history books. All of this is to say that some of the people discussed at the outset of this chapter are peers of the characters in the previous chapter on the Renaissance, and could have easily been discussed there. After all, the Scientific Revolution, though often discussed as a separate event from the Renaissance, was unfolding during and immediately after it. Nevertheless, as the sixteenth century slowly gave way to the seventeenth, the ideas germinated during that time became the basis for the Age of Enlightenment (1685 - 1815 CE).

Also known as the Neoclassical Era or the Age of Reason, philosophy at this time is said to be entering the "modern age." Much like Renaissance philosophy was preoccupied with politics, humanism, and the scientific workings of nature, philosophy during the Age of Reason was largely divided into two schools of thought: empiricism and rationalism.

Empiricism tends to favor the idea that knowledge is directly derived from the senses using one's powers of observation. The work of Renaissance doctor Vesalius could be considered empirical. Rationalism, on the other hand, argues that knowledge comes through intellectual reasoning, much like Galileo's mathematical work. There was a general tug-of-war between these two camps through most of the 17th and 18th centuries, and it would take the work of Immanuel Kant near the dawn of the 19th century to reconcile the two.

Sir Francis Bacon (1561 - 1626 CE) of England was a leading empiricist of the day. Empiricism was quite popular among British intellectuals, with aforementioned fellow countryman Thomas Hobbes also favoring empirical methods within his philosophy. Educated at Trinity College in Cambridge, Bacon developed a strong dislike for Aristotelian philosophy, seeing it as relatively useless. He was, instead, fascinated by reshaping the educational system around scientific knowledge. Philosophy, in his mind, was the technique of reasoning that would cement natural science in education. Reasoning, in the eyes of Bacon, was an empirical experience, based on what each person experiences rather than the utilization of intellectual skills. As he noted in his 1620 work *Novum Organum*, "we have as yet no natural philosophy that is pure…the true business of philosophy must be…to apply the understanding…to a fresh examination of particulars."

He believed that the way forward for science was in experimentation and meticulous data collection. This allowed him to develop different generalizations and laws about the world around him. Mostly, he is remembered for his deep devotion to the belief that experimentation is the only way to gain knowledge.

However, it is not the empiricists who are honored as the forefathers of modern philosophy. That distinction is reserved for René Descartes (1596 - 1650 CE), a staunch rationalist and the creator of the dominant philosophy of the late 17th century. Born in La Haye, Touraine, France (now referred to as Indre-et-Loire), he was a world-class mathematician, a scientist, and of course, a groundbreaking philosopher. He came from a wealthy family and inherited a noble rank from his father. Two short years after his birth, the Wars of Religion (1562 - 1598 CE) formally ended with the Edict of Nantes (1598 CE) which established freedom of religion throughout France. However, tensions and hostilities between Protestants and Catholics continued through Descartes' early lifetime and directly contributed to the Thirty Years' War (1618 - 1648 CE) which was the backdrop for most of Descartes' working life.

Educated at one of the finest schools in Europe, Descartes soon questioned the methods of his teachers, particularly Aristotelian philosophy and Scholasticism, and thus began his long journey of questioning everything. He rejected the empirical notion that all knowledge could be acquired by the senses, arguing that human experience can be quite unreliable. He introduced this idea of doubt, and it motivated him to search for truth and prove facts via reasoning, not observation. His greatest works, authored during the twenty years from 1629 to 1649, are *Le Monde, Discourse on Method, Meditations,* and *Principles of Philosophy.* In these works, he outlined his rationalist philosophy: knowledge can only be gained through reason–if there is any doubt, then an idea should be rejected. As he notes in *Meditations:*

All that up to the present time I have accepted as most true and certain I have learned from the senses or through the senses; but it is sometimes proved to me that these senses are deceptive, and it is wiser not to trust entirely anything by which we have once been deceived.

From this, Descartes arrived at his well-known proof of his own existence, "Je pense, donc je suis." In English, this is "I think, therefore I am," or more famously in Latin, "Cogito ergo sum." He also notes that he can prove his existence through the certainty of numbers; two plus two always equals four.

Although earlier philosophers had discussed the mind and the body as being made of two separate materials or having distinct differences, Descartes was also the first philosopher to establish a modern take on mind-body duality. The mind thinks while the body is a physical occupier of space, and in Descartes' mind, the mind could exist without the body.

Additionally, though Descartes' philosophies were accused of leading to atheism and four of his books were banned by the Catholic Church, Descartes himself retained his belief in God, and his ontological proof of the existence of the self is similar to the Anselmian argument for God. Knowing that his existence was ephemeral, Descartes believed a perfect, immortal, and eternal God existed. He posited that he couldn't have invented or thought of God by himself, so then God must exist. His philosophies, called Cartesianism, dominated the intellectual circles of Europe for the remainder of the 17th century. Considered stylish and popular among the noble classes, Cartesianism blended the religious tastes of the Middle Ages with the scientific discoveries of the Renaissance. Yet, perhaps what Descartes is most remembered for is his skeptical approach and his lifelong dedication to seeking the truth. This kind of individualistic journey for knowledge inspired philosophy and Western thinkers for centuries to come.

The tendency toward individualism that began with Descartes continued with Benedict de Spinoza (also referred to as Baruch Spinoza or Bento de Espinosa) (1632 - 1677 CE). Born in Amsterdam and raised in a Portuguese-Jewish community in Holland, he was incredibly bright. Excommunicated from his Jewish community at the young age of 24, he left Amsterdam and put Judaism behind him. His work was thoroughly inspired by Cartesian principles but he intermingled these with elements of Greek Stoicism, Hobbesian mechanism, and medieval Jewish thought. For Spinoza, philosophy was not some overarching idea that should govern a whole world or nation, rather, it was a personal quest for wisdom born out of a desire to seek human perfection.

His best-known work, *Ethics*, lays out a universe in which God is not the divine creator above all else, predestined to rule. He embraced a monistic view instead; the universe is made of one eternal substance, and this substance is God, noting "Except God, no substance can be or be conceived." This was a large break in tradition for Western philosophers, and Western theism. Until Spinoza, God was largely seen as an entity that was separate from the universe, His creation. Ultimately, Spinoza thought that the highest level of knowledge man can achieve comes in the merging of the transitory individual with the great everlasting substance of the universe.

So while Descartes was a dualist and Spinoza was a monist, a pluralistic form of rationalism exists in the philosophy of Gottfried Wilhelm Leibniz (1646 - 1716 CE). Leibniz, though a valuable philosopher, was firstly a formidable mathematician. He is credited with the invention of differential and integral calculus. This is also attributed to his peer, Sir Isaac Newton (1643 - 1727 CE), and indeed, the pair developed these two branches of mathematics around the same time, completely independent of one another. Serving also as a jurist, historian, diplomat, and librarian, he was an incredibly learned and busy man, and his philosophy is said to be one of the more creative of its ilk.

Mainly interested in logic as a result of his conquests in calculus, he distinguished between two different kinds of truths humanity is capable of understanding: truths of reason and truths of fact. Truths of reason are inevitable, and their opposite cannot possibly exist, while truths of fact are mutable with the potential existence of feasible opposites.

As mentioned earlier, Leibniz provided an alternative to both Descartes and Spinoza with his pluralism. He hypothesized that everything in the universe contains a "mind-like substance" called a monad. These monads all perceive the universe and reflect the universe from their point of view. They are Leibniz's basic substance of the universe. Beyond this thought, his work had much in common with Descartes and Spinoza, particularly their tendency towards hyper-rationalism. This quote from Leibniz's 1714 work *Principes de la nature et de la grâce fondés et raison (Principles of Nature and Grace Founded in Reason)* neatly encapsulates the rationalistic thought of the era:

> True reasoning depends upon necessary or eternal truths, such as those of logic, numbers, geometry,

which establish an indubitable connection of ideas and unfailing consequences.

As the Scientific Revolution of the 16th and 17th centuries gave way to the Age of Enlightenment, philosophers were less bound by religion, or the various universities where they may have learned or taught. In fact, many of the philosophers at this time avoided affiliation with major universities, finding the still-present Scholasticism and Aristotelianism distasteful and woefully misinformed. The age of the saint-philosopher was over, and these new thinkers of the 17th, 18th, and 19th centuries were more defined by socio-economic status than by any other metric. These were noblemen, lawyers, courtiers, diplomats, scholars, and men of leisure. Many educated the ruling classes, like Descartes with Queen Christina of Sweden or Leibniz with the Electress Sophia Charlotte of Prussia. So, despite the advent of the printing press and the general spread of knowledge that occurred during the Renaissance, philosophy remained the property of the wealthy elite. The only difference was that the elite was no longer deeply affiliated with the Roman Catholic Church.

The fathers of the Enlightenment are typically considered to be the Englishmen Sir Isaac Newton and John Locke (1632 - 1704 CE). Newton's work rested on a pinnacle built by the likes of Galileo and Kepler and included his application of mathematics to every facet of nature. Since the 1500s, scientists and philosophers alike had been attempting to unlock nature's secrets, and with Newton's ability to use reason to seemingly conquer the natural world, it looked like the efforts of Bacon, Hobbes, Descartes, and more had finally come to fruition. At this time, though rationalism was still employed, empiricism and the human experience were taken into greater account. While the continental philosophers had dominated the mainstream ideas in the Renaissance and the Scientific Revolution, during the Enlightenment, British empiricists like Locke, George Berkeley (1685 - 1753 CE), and David Hume (1711 - 1776 CE) held the greatest popularity until the Prussian-born Kant toward the second half of the 18th century.

The supremacy of this kind of reason dominated the late 17th and 18th centuries, but philosophers still questioned where reason itself originated from and how the mathematical tenets that seemed to rule the universe could be applied to human nature. In John Locke's *An Essay Concerning Human Understanding*, he tried to tackle the first question. He concluded that human ideas are derived from various sensory experiences and that all thought or "mental operations" come from building more complex concepts out of the basic sensory input that is received. The mind receives primary qualities like motion and density from the senses and then secondary qualities like color or smell are produced by the mind in response to the primary qualities.

Berkeley, who came after Locke, did not agree with this duality of primary and secondary qualities, arguing that all of Locke's primary qualities could be broken down into various secondary qualities. Eventually, Berkeley's rabid empiricism led him to reject abstract ideas, arguing that only what humans can perceive is real. This essentially, in Berkeley's mind, reduced everything in the world down to groups of various sensory qualities. As he said in his 1710 *Treatise Concerning the Principles of Human Knowledge*, "Esse est percipi" (to be is to be perceived). These ideas make him the father of phenomenalism, a school of thought that still influences British philosophical thinkers.

Like Locke and Berkeley, Hume believed that knowledge arises from humanity's sensory experiences. However, unlike Locke and Berkeley, who seemed content that the mind was what it was, Hume took things a step further, triggering a bit of a skeptical crisis. He argued that any similarities between experiences that humans can use to "classify" things simply arise from an associating quality that lives within the mind. Furthermore, the mind itself is not an independent entity like Locke, Berkeley, and hundreds of other intellectuals assumed it to be; rather, it is a "bundle of perceptions" with no real unifying qualities.

Hume's work essentially flew in the face of his era's philosophical thought that put nature in order and honored the human ability to reason. He believed instead that emotions and passions hold greater sway than reason over the individual, noting that "reason is and ought only to be the slave of the passions." Reason, in Hume's mind, only came into play later in an individual's experience to help bolster an idea that they already felt was either acceptable or abominable. Additionally, he argued that if you want to change someone's mind, it would be far easier to appeal to their emotions rather than employing pure, unadulterated logic This resulted in his espousal of religious tolerance; he saw religion as a logical error since, in his mind, there was no clear logical argument for God. Thus, those who practice other religions are not making a logical error, but rather operating from an emotional decision, so why not leave them in peace? In contrast to Descartes, who believed that everything that wasn't rational had to be eliminated, Hume pointed out that very few human behaviors can actually be considered "rational."

Aside from the epistemological advances made by the British empiricists, there was a good deal of political and social philosophy in this period that built off the ideas spawned during the Renaissance. The two most influential texts were Locke's Two *Treatises of Civil Government* and Jean-Jacques Rousseau's *The Social Contract*. These ideas proved to be particularly dominant and led to two major upheavals in the second half of the 18th century: the American Revolution (1775 - 1784 CE) and the French Revolution (1789 - 1799 CE).

Where Machiavelli and Hobbes had assumed the divine right of kings, throwing themselves and their philosophies on the altar of absolutism, Locke and Rousseau were more interested in the people. Freedom and equality of citizens were continual themes, echoing the socio-political change around them as monarchies lost the strength they had enjoyed for so long, giving way to more democratic structures. The Glorious Revolution of 1688 limited the authoritative power of the British Crown, and across Europe, people were becoming increasingly dissatisfied with their continual mistreatment at the hands of their monarchs.

Locke expressly repudiated the divine right of kings, arguing that freedom and equality were natural rights granted to humanity. In contrast to the Hobbesian idea of man's natural state being horrifying anarchy, Locke instead thought that it was simply in humanity's best interests to band together and form governments. However, this political contract should be invested in the preservation of "life, liberty, and property." Many will note the similarities between this line and Thomas Jefferson's famous line in the American Declaration of Independence that declares "life, liberty, and the pursuit of happiness" to be the core inalienable rights of man. Jefferson was, as were many of the American Founding Fathers, heavily influenced by the ideas of Locke.

Instead of just accepting that humanity was meant to be ruled over by a select few, Locke instead believed there is no legitimate governmental power without the consent of the governed. However, once that relationship has been established, then people must acquiesce to what the majority of the citizenry decides.

Rousseau was heavily influenced by Locke, agreeing with his idea that a social contract is a basis for a lawful government. Yet, Rousseau's ideas fell along more collectivist lines than Lockean principles did. Chief among these was the concept that individual rights are inferior to the general will of society. The goal of the state should always be the freedom and equality of its citizens, and if the people find their government to be in breach of that contract, then they are morally compelled to revolt and overthrow their unjust rulers.

Though they had some differences, the writings of both Locke and Rousseau established the bedrock on which all representative democracies in the West were built.

As previously mentioned, philosophy before the second half of the 18th century had strayed away from the citadels of learning in Europe and embedded itself among the upper crust of society. As the 1700s continued, philosophy gradually became a profession, rather than a hobby of the well-to-do dilettante. The discipline also became more and more accessible to varying social classes as philosophers gradually began to return to the universities, starting with the University of Halle in Germany.

The Enlightenment in Germany had seen the philosophers return to the universities much earlier than the rest of Europe, and as a result, they were the first region to have philosophy specialists and professionals. Along with professorships, professional journals, an invention of the 17th century, dedicated to philosophy began to circulate. German thinkers also produced many written histories of philosophy at this time as well.

Amid all this growth sprang up Immanuel Kant. Considered the best of all modern philosophers and an apex in the Enlightenment, Kant was a German from Königsberg, Prussia (now Kaliningrad, Russia) with a modest background. Educated at the University of Königsberg, he became enamored with the work of Sir Isaac Newton. Kant is most lauded for his philosophical ability to thread the needle between the hardline rationalists like Leibniz and the dedicated empiricists like Hume. Kant established a new definition for the field of philosophy, created a brand new philosophical method, and instituted a new structure for philosophical texts and treatises.

Reason, for Kant, was the core of any philosophical thought. Kant was so dedicated to reason that he hoped to supplant the traditional religious ethics and morals with those governed by human reason alone. He called this a "categorical imperative," which is essentially a restatement of the old Golden Rule: "do unto others as you would have them do unto you." He wasn't much of a religious man, but he did recognize the moral clarity that religion supplied. Hoping philosophy could eventually meet this need, his definition was as follows, "[Philosophy] is the science of the relation of all knowledge to the essential ends of human reason." The job of the philosopher is to determine what is true knowledge derived from reason and what is simply a mirage masquerading as reason. Philosophers must test the bounds of human reason, and to do this, Kant employed a specific method.

Kant called this his "transcendental" or "critical" method. He rejected any pure dogmatism and favored the skepticism espoused by his predecessor, Descartes. He fought the notion that objects in the universe have to adhere to human reason and instead argued that it is knowledge and reason that must adapt around them, much like Copernicus showed with his heliocentric model that conflicted with the assumed geocentric model of his day.

However, unlike Descartes, Kant was certain that knowledge existed. What he wanted to figure out instead was how knowledge was possible and how it was structured. In three separate critiques, written in 1781, 1788, and 1790, Kant set out to examine reason in three different ways it is used in the human mind. In his first work, the *Critique of Pure Reason*, he delved into the idea of reason in thinking, or how reason is used in science. In his next, the *Critique of Practical Reason*, Kant scrutinized reason in the will or the use of reason in ethical decisions. Finally, in the *Critique of Judgment*, he discussed reason in feeling or aesthetics.

With these critiques, Kant introduced a new literary form to the field of philosophy. The dialogues favored by Plato and the wordy treatises enjoyed by medieval scholars were still in use, but Kant originated the critique. He used this technique in all three of his critiques, separating the text into three sections. The first would cover an analysis of reason ("analytic"), the second section was an exercise in logic, showing where errors might be made ("dialectic"), while the third and final section laid out the rules through which one should practice ("methodology").

With Kant's death occurring near the end of the Enlightenment to a close in 1804, it is fitting that his philosophy, though largely an attempt to secularize the morality of religion, was also a synthesis of the rationalist and empiricist schools that had split the philosophical community throughout the era. Kant believed that the rationalists were right by assuming some things can be known a priori, while the empiricists were right to assert that knowledge can arise out of experience. The combination of these two schools of thought taught that knowledge can be acquired in both ways, not just one or the other. This greatly influenced the philosophical notion of transcendental idealism, which became a prevalent philosophy in the 19th century, impacting the philosophies of Georg Wilhelm Friedrich Hegel (1770 - 1831 CE) and Friedrich Nietzsche (1844 - 1900 CE).

With the conclusion of the Age of Reason, philosophy had returned to the universities and was more widely available to the masses. Now recognized as a distinct discipline and profession all on its own, it was divorced from religion, and the world itself was far more secular. Yet as the 19th century dawned, more change was just around the corner. Technological advancements, changes in world powers, and the explosion of urban life would come with the Industrial Age, taking philosophy right along with it.

7

REASON, ROMANTICISM, AND RIDICULOUSNESS IN THE INDUSTRIAL AGE (1815 - 1900 CE)

U p until the 19th century, philosophy had largely been torn between two opposing schools of thought or several different doctrines. However, in the 1800s, like the proliferation of technology, philosophies seemed to spring up everywhere with diverse ideas. There were many rivals and warring factions: positivism against irrationalism, pragmatism versus idealism, and in the political realm, Marxism stood against liberalism. Yet, if one major philosophical achievement is to be highlighted in this era, it is the development of irrationalism.

Within the culture and society of Europe, as well as within the newly-minted United States, changes were afoot. The Romantic Movement, which was largely a reaction to the hyper-focused dedication the last century had towards reason, favored feelings above all else. One can think of the poetry of Shelley, Byron, and Keats or the paintings of Friedrich, Goya, and Gericault to get an idea of the cultural flavor of the day. This century saw the impact of the Industrial Revolution (1760 - 1840 CE) which created untold wealth for some but poverty and destitution for many more. The Revolutions of 1848 changed political perspectives, advocating for greater liberty and democracy in France, the Italian states, the German states, the Hapsburg Empire, and elsewhere. Finally, the work of Charles Darwin (1809 - 1882 CE) had a massive impact on science, but also echoed into the halls of philosophy. The combining threads of Romanticism, social unrest, technological advancements, and massive economic inequality drove the philosophy of the age.

Inspired by Kant, Leibniz, and Spinoza, the German idealists were the dominating philosophical force of the early 19th century. This was, however, a much more spiritualistic bent of idealism than Kant had espoused. Due in part to the rise of Romanticism in art and literature, German idealism was also influenced by religion. Ironic, since Kant had striven to create a secular moral code apart from faith. Most of the leading voices of the German idealist school were either former theology students or sons of Protestant pastors. It is likely this somber, Protestant influence that gave German idealism its intensely serious nature.

The chief voices of this particular philosophical movement were Johann Fichte (1764 - 1814 CE) and Georg Wilhelm Friedrich Hegel. In a departure from their predecessor, Kant, these men believed the primary goal of philosophy is to understand the self, self-consciousness, and the greater universe as a whole.

Fichte, a professor at the University of Berlin, wove elements of Descartes, Spinoza, and of course, Kant, into his thought processes. From Descartes he borrowed a general sense of subjectivism, he folded in Spinoza's monistic concept of the universe and placed it all under a Kantian moral framework. He elevated philosophy, making it the highest of all intellectual pursuits since, in his mind, it is the "clarification of consciousness." In short, Fichte thought that philosophers would have the highest level of self-consciousness among all humanity, believing that only they could see the core of reality: the "Mind" (also called the "Spirit").

Hegel expanded on this line of thought, and he is widely acknowledged as one of the greatest thinkers of his century, despite his notoriously abstruse writing.

Much like Kant, Hegel desired to find reason's place within nature, but where Kant had seen reason as something humans place upon the world, Hegel believed instead that reason was gradually discovered by mankind. Hegel also taught that knowledge was not necessarily derived from an expected place.

In his mind, mankind's progress was never linear, so every era of history had something valuable that could be learned and brought into the present. The story of man was not a direct line from brutish ignorance to glittering intelligence, but rather a convoluted crossroads of peaks and valleys. Progress, in Hegel's eyes, is messy and it takes time to strike the right balance as a society. He dubbed this evolution the "dialectical process," arguing that it takes three moves to reach a solution: the thesis, the antithesis, and the synthesis. Additionally, it is prudent for people to study ideas they dislike, not only ones that confirm previously held beliefs. This is a way to test one's principles for clarity and rightness. Reason for Hegel is not some eternal, clear entity, but is instead "historical" and ever-evolving.

While the German philosophers of the 19th century were busy pretending that empiricism had never prevailed in philosophical thought, the French and English intellectuals were gladly upholding the tradition. Auguste Comte (1798 - 1857 CE), born in Montpellier, France, is considered the founder of positivist philosophy, though inklings of positivist thought can be seen as far back as the ancient Greeks. Deeply inspired by the works of the British empiricists, particularly Bacon, Comte put forth a rigid philosophy that rejected all types of knowledge except the knowledge gained through scientific study. Esteemed as the first philosopher of science in the modern era, Comte argued that science had progressed linearly throughout human history, beginning with mathematics and ending with sociology. He also posited a "law of three stages," which describes every academic field as moving from superstition to science by beginning with religion, moving on to metaphysical thought, and ending with scientific thought. He initiated a strong turn against religion and metaphysics that persisted into the 20th century.

Meanwhile, in England, John Stuart Mill (1806 - 1873), continued the work of his predecessors Bacon, Berkeley, and Hume. He was, like Comte, distrustful of metaphysical philosophy, and his work the *Examination of Sir William Hamilton's Philosophy* demonstrated this distrust while neatly congealing the philosophies of Berkeley and Hume. In his later work, *A System of Logic*, Mill lays out his scientific methodology and delineates the differences between inductive and deductive reasoning.

It is, however, Mill's social views that are more interesting. Like Comte who believed that sociology was the pinnacle of science, Mill also believed that true social science was a plausible possibility. An adherent of Locke and Rousseau, Mill fervently believed in liberalism, and he came to represent the most extreme version of it in the 19th century, standing diametrically opposed to German-born Karl Marx (1818 - 1883 CE). He saw the negative effects of the Industrial Revolution, and his ethics are outlined in his 1861 work *Utilitarianism*. Inspired by Jeremy Bentham, the founder of utilitarianism, which champions the greatest good for the greatest number, Mill gave Bentham's social ideas a more individualistic cast. Fearful of the "tyranny of the majority," Mill advocated absolute freedom in speech and thought. In his eyes, no institution or government has the right to inhibit a person's development. He advocated for social reforms, and representation for minority figures in his society, while warning others about the dangers of legislation that directly benefits one class or group of people.

On the other side of the socio-political coin lay Karl Marx. Born in Trier, Germany on the Luxembourg border, Marx was influenced by Hegel and more surprisingly, by Rousseau. Disgusted by the treatment of workers that he witnessed during the Industrial

Revolution, Marx questioned the aims of a capitalist society built on profit maximization. In 1848, he published *The Communist Manifesto*, which was co-written with Friedrich Engels (1820 - 1895 CE). Within the work, he called for a forceful overthrow of the social order of the day, arguing that history demonstrated a pattern of a wealthy minority exploiting a more economically vulnerable majority. The recent minority and majority he alluded to were the bourgeoisie and the proletariat, respectively. He believed that the proletariat should form a Communist Party to protect their interests and keep the bourgeoisie from controlling society. From there a just and fair socialist society could develop and flourish. Marx is best remembered for being a political firebrand, and his idea of history being a long story of humanity locked into a class struggle has endured into the present day.

As the nineteenth century progressed, Hegel's work, seen largely as a bridge from the Enlightenment over into the modern era, was called to question by the work of the irrationalists. Hegel had, understandably given his proximity to the Enlightenment, believed quite firmly in the capabilities of human rationality, and this had largely remained unquestioned until the work of Søren Kierkegaard (1813 - 1855 CE), Arthur Schopenhauer (1788 - 1860 CE), and of course, Friedrich Nietzsche (1844 - 1900 CE).

A native of Copenhagen, Denmark, Kierkegaard mocked Hegelian philosophy for being blind to the actualities of daily human life. He saw Hegel's work as overly pretentious and ignorant of the emotions and whims of the individual. Endlessly questioning the world is not the way forward in Kierkegaard's mind, but rather making strong decisions and standing by them. The crux of humanity is not found in the rational mind, but in the emotional storm of existence, namely in the emotional experiences of anxiety and despair. Even the titles of his works betray a preoccupation with these emotions: *Fear and Trembling, The Concept of Dread,* and *The Sickness Unto Death.*

Often crowned the "father of existentialism," Kierkegaard emphasized an individual's existence and how that played into religion. As a Christian, he saw his faith not as a set of rules to follow, but as a way of life. His philosophy inspired 20th-century Protestant theology and widely influenced literature. He rebelled against the popular notion that "becoming your highest self" was easy to achieve, arguing instead that the slog for individual righteousness is an infinite one.

Schopenhauer, a fellow countryman and contemporary of Hegel's, contradicted the Hegelian assertion that the irrational wasn't real. Often referred to as the "philosopher of pessimism" in contrast to Hegel's idealism, Schopenhauer embraced the Kantian idea that what humanity can perceive is ruled by space, time, and causality, but he also believed that science could not dig below the surface of this world of appearances.

The world, according to Schopenhauer, is governed by a strong cosmic Will that expresses itself in human instinct, the wildness of nature, and animal behavior. Rationality and clarity are in short supply in this real world, and impulse, conflict, and hardship are things that science cannot touch. As he noted in his work *On the Suffering of the World*, "If the immediate and direct purpose of our life is not suffering then our existence is the most ill-adapted to its purpose in the world." Science and reason to Schopenhauer are not the core realities of the world. That distinction belongs to the daily conflicts and impulses humans encounter.

Nietzsche, a mustachioed, quirky man from Röcken, Germany, generally agreed with Schopenhauer's assessment that the human mind is ruled by instinct. As a philosopher, he saw it as his duty to tear down antiquated standards of behavior and build a better civilization from their ruins. In his mind, the two greatest roadblocks to the progress of Western culture were Christianity and alcohol, believing that both dulled the senses and kept people comfortable with the status quo.

Though chronically ill and in pain, he was not satisfied with accepting life as it was, and his work strove to expose the motivations behind the accepted traditions of religion, morality, and philosophy. In his early work, Nietzsche was heavily influenced by Schopenhauer and Romantic artists, particularly the composer Richard Wagner (1813 - 1883 CE). Works like *The Birth of Tragedy* (1872) stem from this period in his life. Ultimately estranged from Wagner and mildly disillusioned with the philosophies of Schopenhauer, Nietzsche went the opposite direction, praising reason and science in books like *Human, All Too Human* (1878), and *The Gay Science* (1882). However, it is in works like *Thus Spoke Zarathustra* (1883), *Twilight of the Idols* (1888), and *The Antichrist* (1888) that his mature philosophy is truly seen.

He was critical of traditional morality, believing that good and bad should not necessarily be seen as descriptors of moral value. He was fascinated by the emotional impulses of humanity, and frequently disgusted by the way Christian theology urged its adherents to squash their instincts, especially those of pride and envy which he believed could be positively wielded. In the end, Nietzsche suffered a mental break and spent the last eleven years unable to care for himself. First residing in an asylum, he was later released to his mother, and then his sister. After he died in 1900, much of his work was twisted by his sister and unfortunately became associated with fascism and the rise of Adolf Hitler, though this is a gross misapplication of his ideas.

Due to his unfair linkage with the famous 2oth century dictator and his tendency to make iconoclastic pronouncements like, "God is dead... And we have killed him," Nietzsche is often misunderstood and mischaracterized. Much like Kierkegaard and Schopenhauer, he was fascinated by the irrationalities of the human mind, and the complex emotional landscapes experienced by man. The three of them together brought philosophy into the 20th century with their literary abilities–rescuing philosophy from what they saw as the sterile halls of academia and bringing it out into the world of art and entertainment.

The influence of the irrationalists, particularly Nietzsche, reaches deep into the 20th century. The German and French philosophers like Martin Heidegger (1889 - 1976 CE), Jacques Derrida (1930 - 2004 CE), and Michel Foucault (1926 - 1984 CE) and their associated schools of deconstructionism and existentialism owe much to the ideas posited by the 19th-century irrationalists. Psychologists, novelists, poets, and playwrights alike all cite Nietzsche as an influence. His ideas would spark in the minds of some of the best-remembered luminaries of the twentieth century like Sigmund Freud (1856 - 1939 CE), George Bernard Shaw (1856 - 1950 CE), and Rainer Maria Rilke (1875 - 1926 CE).

8

THE ANALYTIC AND THE CONTINENTAL - DEVELOPMENTS IN TWENTIETH AND TWENTY-FIRST CENTURIES (1900 - 2022 CE)

Throughout Western history, philosophy has been the purview and the plaything of learned men. What changed was who these learned men were. In Greece and Rome, they were from wealthy families, like Plato and Democritus (though Socrates is a notable exception). Medieval Europe elevated religious men to the rank of the philosopher, often commingling the philosophers and theologians. In the Renaissance and the Age of Enlightenment, the philosophers were frequently men from noble families with the leisure and connections to devote their lives to the craft. By the time of Kant, "philosopher" was a recognized profession, and philosophy became enshrined at centers of higher learning throughout the Western world.

However, even in the 19th century, though Hegel and the idealist school of thought remained shackled to academia, many of the greatest and most remembered philosophers were not professors associated with any university.

Yet, in the 21st century, philosophy is seen as the pastime of the collegiate elite, filled with introspective navel-gazing that can only be tolerated in the ivory towers of academia. It is a popular trope in 21st-century America to lampoon those who pursue philosophy as a college degree, deeming them "worthless" in the eyes of the general public. The missing piece between the 19th and 21st-century treatment of philosophy, naturally, is the 20th century. Throughout the 20th century, philosophy trended toward more and more academic tendencies. The foremost philosophers were professors, writing in complicated vocabulary. Their target audiences were their peers, not the general public. The problems they addressed were not larger intellectual concerns, but smaller, more particular issues. As a result, the differences between philosophical schools of thought have sharpened, as have the arguments over the definition of philosophy. Philosophy now tends to look inward at itself, rather than outward to answer life's questions.

A turbulent and destructive one hundred years, the 20th century claimed countless lives and is marked as one of the bloodiest in human history. As a result of the violent and divisive conflicts that tore through the European continent, Western philosophy largely fractured along geographical and cultural differences. English-speaking nations, spearheaded by the United States and the United Kingdom, continued to follow the Lockean tradition of clear logic and analysis, in keeping with their empirical ancestors. On the mainland, the theoretical legacy of Hegel lived on, though the actual belief systems of his successors veered wildly away from his initial ideas. Over time, this schism of Western thought gave rise to two stylistically different philosophical approaches: the "analytic" and the "Continental," respectively. They remained largely distinct until the last decade of the 2oth century.

Aside from analytic and Continental thought, there were two other movements of note during this century. The work of Henri Bergson (1859 - 1941 CE), Alfred North Whitehead (1861 - 1947 CE), and John Dewey (1859 - 1952 CE), though distinctly different from one another, all engage in a type of speculative philosophy that is not easy to categorize. The second movement is the proliferation of Marxist philosophical practices that began in the earlier half of the 20th century.

Bergson, a French philosopher who influenced later French thinkers like Jean-Paul Sartre (1905 - 1980 CE), enjoyed a fair bit of popularity until the conclusion of World War II (1939 - 1945 CE). He is notable for refining different ways of knowing, similar to how Kant tried to reconcile the rationalists and the empiricists a century earlier. Bergson delineated the difference between knowledge gained through analysis, which is crucial to the field of science, and knowledge gained through intuition. For Bergson, this knowledge of intuition came from an ability to utilize one's intellect to have sympathy for and identify with other organisms. It is through this intuition that a person can discover their essence which he called *la durée* (the duration).

Despite the Kantian-like way in which he distinguishes knowledge, his work *Time and Free Will: An Essay on the Immediate Data of Consciousness* is largely seen as an attack on Kant. Interestingly enough, it is also said to be what inspired Sartre's interest in philosophy. Here he also outlines his best-remembered concept: multiplicity. The concept is arduous to grasp, but in short, it is seen as a way to combine the ideas of heterogeneity and continuity.

Whitehead, too, was interested in the metaphysical realm of philosophy and saw it as the main thrust of the discipline. An English philosopher largely known more as a mathematician before he emigrated to the United States, Whitehead tried to develop a logical system of ideas. He rejected the traditional split between the objective world (facts, science, et cetera) and the subjective world (art, religion, and more) and tried to find harmony between the two through his philosophy. As he wrote, "Philosophy attains its chief importance by fusing the two, namely, religion and science, into one rational scheme of thought."

Unlike Bergson and Whitehead, preoccupied with metaphysical thought, Dewey, an American, was more interested in philosophy as a whole and how the different aspects of the discipline interacted with one another. A leading light for American pragmatism, Dewey argued that the role of the philosopher was not to garner professional distinction but to be of service to humanity. Seeing the massive social, economic, and cultural troubles of the 20th century, Dewey saw philosophy as an answer to them, believing that continuous intelligent social planning could produce the kind of change necessary to end the strife. If philosophy were to guide public policy, Dewey believed that the goals and desires of a democratic nation could be more effectively realized. His work is often lauded as the first political philosophy spawned by a modern liberal democracy.

Aside from Dewey's political inklings, there was another politically motivated philosophical movement that dominated the 20th century: Marxism. The philosophy was, as the name suggests, chiefly inspired by the framework laid down by Marx in the 19th century, though it did have some additions gifted to it by Vladimir Lenin (1870 - 1924 CE). Though it began in the Soviet Union and was propagated by its satellite states in the Eastern Bloc of Europe, it spread into all of Europe and the Americas throughout the 20th century.

Much like the pragmatist thought in the United States, Marxism was dedicated to the practical application of theoretical ideas. Theory was all well and good, but both Marx and Lenin agreed that it was simply a transformative tool for the initiation of the class struggle needed to further the goals of the proletariat. As a result, Marxist philosophy is virtually indistinguishable from Marxist ideology, and that is no accident.

As Marxism migrated westward, two different factions emerged: those dedicated to the traditional ideas and politics associated with Marxism and Leninism and those that diffused it into leftist thought in the second half of the century. The latter class of individuals is identified as "Western Marxists," and it was primarily induced by the overall failure of socialist revolutions in the West. Western Marxism is mostly interested in the philosophical implications of Marxist theory, not so much the political or economic practices. Notable Western Marxists include György Lukács (1885 - 1971 CE) of Hungary, Antonio Gramsci (1891 - 1937 CE) of Italy, Jean-Paul Sartre and Maurice Merleau-Ponty (1908 - 1961 CE) of France, and members of the Frankfurt School in Germany–particularly Max Horkheimer (1895 - 1937 CE) and Herbert Marcuse (1898 - 1979 CE).

These thinkers were mostly absorbed by the historical and cultural impact of Marxism and busied themselves studying alternative, non-Marxist approaches, especially since they lived during a time of capitalistic success. Although orthodox Marxism predicts the ultimate overthrow of the bourgeoisie by the proletariat in a revolution, the Western Marxists witnessed moments in history that Karl Marx would have thought a moment for revolution, but the crises he theorized did not materialize. Their beliefs were further tested by the horrors of Stalinist Russia, so their initial social advocacy was for workers' councils to assume the reins of power and eliminate the professional class of politicians. Later, they emphasized more anarchist principles when the proletariat class seemed too enmeshed with the capitalistic system.

Most Western Marxists were inspired by Marx's early writings which don't have the absolutist, dogmatic slant of his later works. Seen as generally impractical by orthodox Marxists, Western Marxists were usually far-removed from the working class they claimed to represent, and were often members of a more wealthy intellectual elite. Regardless, their outlook on Marxism and the writings and philosophies they produced have colored life all over the world and affected the perception of Marxist teachings.

Marxism on the whole remained influential throughout the 20th century, particularly in Latin America, early 1970s Argentina to be exact, where liberation philosophy was rampant. Liberation philosophy, which took quite a bit from Marxism, was concerned with the needs of the poor in Latin America, viewing them as perpetually oppressed. They believed that there was no current philosophy available that addressed their concerns, and they condemned Western philosophy as stagnant and elitist with little bearing on daily life. Liberation philosophy was popular throughout Latin America, and its influence reached as far as North America and Western Europe.

Returning from the tangential break covering the speculative and political philosophers of the era, the two main branches of philosophy were, as previously noted, analytic and Continental. Analytic philosophers don't necessarily have one unifying school of thought, but they do have similar heritages and approaches to problems, allowing them to easily cluster together in the history books. G.E. Moore (1873 - 1958 CE), a British intellectual, is often highlighted as the originator, laying a baseline analytic thought process down in his *Principia Ethica*. He argued that much of the strife within the philosophical field arises from people trying to answer questions when they aren't sure which question they actually want to answer. Analysis and clarification are needed to provide philosophers with direction, and this idea laid the groundwork for a method of philosophy that is primarily interested in addressing philosophical problems.

It is no accident that the analytic philosophers are primarily from the British tradition–which includes all countries in the Anglosphere like the United States, Canada, Australia, and New Zealand. Empiricism had always flourished in these lands and analytic philosophy is not so far removed from that heritage. The development of symbolic logic within the field of mathematics (the use of symbols to express logical ideas) was a primary influence on analytics at the beginning of the 20th century, as was a field of science.

As a result, many analytic philosophers saw the clear logical progression of math and science as a roadmap for the direction philosophy should follow, though not all completely agreed. Due to this divergence of opinion, analytical philosophers were either interested in using "formal" or logical techniques for analysis while others followed an "informal" or ordinary language method, and some used a combination of the two. For the first seventy-five years of the 20th century, analytics mainly concerned themselves with reference and meaning, but the last twenty-five years saw a decisive shift. From the mid-1970s onward to the turn of the century, analytic philosophers became increasingly preoccupied with analyzing the human mind and human mental processes like judging, believing, or perceiving.

Within both the formalist and informalist schools, there were several different subgroups of importance. For clarity's sake, this text will begin with the formalist school and discuss the subtypes of logical atomism, logical positivism, naturalized epistemology, identity theory, functionalism, and eliminative materialism.

Logical atomism was metaphysical in its interests, championed by the British philosopher Bertrand Russell (1872 - 1970 CE). It was largely adapted from mathematical logic and inspired by the writings of his student, Ludwig Wittgenstein (1889 - 1953 CE). The pair were separated during World War I (1914 - 1918 CE) with Russell in England and Wittgenstein in the Austrian Army, but they appear to largely agree on the major aspects of their theories.

Both men saw mathematics as the underlying fabric of the universe, and that daily life and ordinary language act as a kind of "cloak" covering up the structural realities upon which the world is built. Atomic facts are facts that are "features of reality," fully independent of the mind and making up the objects of the world. These facts are seemingly simple truisms like, the sky is blue, or the grass is green. This theory assumed, realistically, that there are facts in the world that are independent of the human mind. It also assumed that language is dependent on humanity, or some kind of sentient entity that uses symbols to communicate ideas. The finer points of logical atomism faded over time, but Russell and Wittgenstein's assertion that philosophy is the child of science, math, and logic, persisted throughout the century.

Logical positivism, which rose up in the 1920s, accepted the logical atomists' claim that philosophy should be planted firmly in mathematical logic. Mostly propagated by a clique of Austrian intellectuals who called themselves the Wiener Kreis (Vienna Circle), but unlike the logical atomists, these men largely believed that only science and mathematics are capable of making any sound intellectual statements. In their mind, proclamations that came from metaphysical, artistic, religious, or ethical arenas were not credible and deserved little attention from serious philosophers.

This immediately discredited logical atomism in their minds, since this was a form of metaphysical thought. There was a split in their mind between analytic statements that do not necessitate observations and what they referred to as "synthetic statements" that required experiential knowledge. An example of an analytic statement would be "Two halves make a whole" while a synthetic statement would be "The floor is wet."

Notable logical positivists include Rudolf Carnap (1891 - 1970 CE) and Herbert Feigl (1902 - 1988 CE), both of whom, along with their compatriots, fled Germany and Austria for the United States during the Nazi occupation. The arrival of logical positivism on the American continent had a huge impact on American philosophy for the remainder of the 20th century and into the dawn of the 21st.

Willard Van Orman Quine (1908 - 2000 CE), inspired by the work of Russell as well as the logical positivists, particularly Rudolf Carnap, developed his own school of thought and was considered a leader in the field of analytic philosophy up until his death. Quine's philosophy is typically called naturalized epistemology and it agreed with much of the logical positivists' thoughts, though he did not adhere to their idea of the analytic-synthetic statement dichotomy. Developed from his belief that philosophy is an extension of science, much of his work was dedicated to providing psychological answers for the way humans attain scientific knowledge. He saw it as his job to describe how all the major scientific theories about the world are procured through human experience.

As alluded to earlier in the text, the last twenty-five years of the 20th century mostly involved applying the materialist philosophies–mostly logical positivism and naturalized epistemology–of the previous seventy-five years to the inner workings of the human mind. This resulted in three differing theories. The first, identity theory, put forth the idea that the mental experiences of the mind are identical to the physical state of the human brain, essentially saying that the mind and the brain are the same.

The second, functionalism, argues that any internal mental state or thought is the result of the function it plays in a larger system. These thoughts, desires, and internal experiences serve a function within a larger network of sensory experiences and behaviors. To put it simply, in a functionalist's mind, pain exists as an effect of a physical stimulus, like a cut, and causes mental states like fear or anxiety.

The third and final theory is eliminative materialism. This rather stark idea submits that things like belief, intention, or other mental states simply do not exist, there is only neural activity. To an eliminative materialist, if the way the brain operates is fully unmasked, then humanity's entire mental experience could be explained. Referring to belief, intention, and states of mind as "folk psychology," eliminative materialists believe there is no further need for the study of such things in modern science and philosophy, as they are irrelevant.

While the formalist traditions of the analytic philosophers discussed above relied heavily on logic and science, those members of the informalist tradition acknowledged the importance of both but did not see them as viable models to dissect the intellectual problems of the 20th century. Three major perspectives developed: common-sense philosophy, ordinary-language philosophy, and speech-act theory.

Common-sense philosophy was first elucidated in Moore's 1925 paper "A Defense of Common Sense." It was mostly a retort against idealist and skepticist thought processes that were gaining popularity in the United Kingdom during the beginning of the 20th century. Moore, the great godfather of analytic philosophy, railed against the skeptic's notion that no one could know anything to be true, noting that multiple propositions about the world can be deemed true. For example, Moore pointed to the existence of many different human beings over the years and in the present. The statement "many human beings have existed and do exist" can certainly be categorized as true. In response to idealism, the belief that the world is a mental creation, Moore again pointed out the propositions he believes are factually true. If humans have existed and do exist, those are material things. This fact, in Moore's eyes, automatically falsifies the idealist's idea that the material world does not exist. Moore dubbed this perspective the "common sense view of the world," and readily dismissed any philosophical theory that conflicted with it.

Ordinary-language philosophy was the brainchild of Gilbert Ryle (1900 - 1976 CE) and John Langshaw (J.L.) Austin (1911 - 1960 CE), two British philosophers who believed that philosophical problems stem from a misinterpretation of spoken language. For example, in Ryle's *The Concept of the Mind,* he points out that the typical idea of the human mind as an invisible entity within the body is based on one fundamental mistake: the body and the mind are treated as two analogous but distinct entities by human language. The long-held idea of Cartesian dualism (that is that the mind and body are two separate things) was largely destroyed through Ryle's work.

Austin, on the other hand, was more interested in highlighting the importance of language. In his celebrated paper "A Plea for Excuses," Austin dissects the use of language in philosophy, arguing that it is a crucial tool, but that everyday speech needs to–at times–be modified by headier technical concepts. Language and its ability to give humans a tool to highlight distinctions (i.e., telling a friend from a foe) are incredibly important, and according to Austin, philosophy should strive to appeal to ordinary language first.

Austin also had his hand in the development of speech-act theory. Considered one of the most unique philosophies of the 20th century, speech-act theory discusses spoken words that have the same grammatical cast as a statement but is neither true nor false. A common example of this would be saying "I do" in a marriage ceremony. These two words are not inherently true or false, but they are still quite meaningful within their context. Austin named these "performatives," and his work in this arena largely harpooned the positivist notion that every sentence is either true or false, calling it a "descriptive fallacy."

After his death, Austin's student, John R. Searle (b. 1932 CE), an American, continued and refined speech-act theory. His 1995 book *The Construction of Social Reality* points out that many institutions are created through speech acts. He highlights money, as one such institution, created by a governmental decree. Police departments, universities, banks, and many other organizations are established similarly. Searle's work married a philosophy of language into the realms of social and political theory.

Though analytic philosophy remained dominant throughout the Anglosphere, the main continent of Europe persisted in its own traditions, particularly phenomenology and existentialism in the first half of the 20th century. After World War II, the focus shifted mostly to a critical repudiation of metaphysics and rationalism in the face of the horrors of the first half of the century.

Phenomenology, largely created by the German mathematician and intellectual Edmund Husserl (1859 - 1938 CE), is the study of the appearances of things in the universe (the "phenomena") and the way humanity experiences those things. Husserl is mostly remembered in the field for creating the phenomenological method and the "life-world" concept. The phenomenological method is supposed to analyze a conscious experience possible by stripping away any unnecessary metaphysical theories or empirical assumptions. Husserl's idea of a "life-world" is a descriptor of an individual's particular life and experiences, framed with that person at the center. It is the immediate, personal world each person experiences.

Eventually, phenomenology became quite popular, with its most well-known proponent being Martin Heidegger (1889 -1976 CE). Raised as a Roman Catholic in Messkirch, Germany, Heidegger was a student of Husserl's at the University of Freiburg. Ultimately rejecting the faith of his birth after studying the texts of Martin Luther and John Calvin (1509 - 1564 CE), he married a Lutheran woman and went on to work as a lecturer at his alma mater alongside Husserl. Though his reputation has been tarnished by his involvement with the Nazi party, Heidegger remains one of the brightest philosophers of the 20th century. His work mostly involved the adaptation of Husserl's phenomenological approaches to the very core of human existence. He rejected the idea that philosophy was an empirical exercise, and focused instead on philosophy's ability to explore the individual experience of life.

In his seminal masterpiece, *Being and Time*, Heidegger explores principles of human existence, particularly *dasein* (in English, being-there or there being). *Dasein* is a self-conscious awareness of one's existence, a keen recognition of the mystery of human life. His work investigates humanity's existence in the world as well as death and the accompanying fear of "not being." His radical approach to phenomenology and existentialism, as well as his creative use of the German language, made Heidegger one of the most well-known Continental philosophers to date.

Aside from the phenomenological contributions of Husserl and Heidegger, existentialism was the other, larger school of thought among Continental philosophers. Existentialism, with roots in the philosophies of Kierkegaard and Nietzsche, was propelled into the 20th century by the German Karl Jaspers (1883 - 1969 CE) and the Frenchman Jean-Paul Sartre.

Jaspers, who arrived at philosophy after working in the fields of medicine and psychology, was mainly interested in what it meant to exist as a person. Jaspers, like Dewey in the analytic school, had a practical application in mind for philosophy. The aim of the discipline, in Jaspers' mind, should be the revelation of "Being." This can be found through universal but intense human experiences like death, suffering, and conflict. When an individual butts up against these moments in their life, it is at that moment that they encounter what human existence truly means.

Sartre, like Jaspers, was preoccupied with "Being" and the existential dread that humanity experiences when confronting their mortality. However, Sartre framed the core of Being around freedom. He believed that self-determination and freedom of choice were the keys to discovering authenticity. A prolific writer and celebrated playwright, Sartre hailed from Paris, where he spent the majority of his life. His 1943 work, *Being and Nothingness*, with its inscrutable ideas made him a household name in the Western world and greatly popularized existentialism.

His views on the inherent absurdity of the world and the freedom humans should enjoy struck at the heart of determinism; every person, in Sartre's mind, is just making it up as they go, there is no predetermined path or fate for individuals or indeed for humanity as a whole. He believed that those who told themselves they had to be, act, or do things a certain way were living in "bad faith." However, this absolute freedom could cause a kind of anguish. As he said in *Being and Nothingness* and later elaborated on during a 1946 lecture entitled "Existentialism is a Humanism," "Man is condemned to be free; because once thrown into the world, he is responsible for everything he does." There is no blaming anyone else in Sartre's mind, though he does make allowances for certain pre-existing economic and social conditions, viewing them as legitimate obstacles to freedom.

Sartre's work after World War II addresses these obstacles to freedom more directly. Before the war, he had acknowledged structural difficulties to attaining absolute freedom but had insisted that people needed to continuously strive to overcome these obstacles. In his 1960 work, *Critique of Dialectical Reason,* Sartre conceded that he had been mistaken, ignoring social justice issues in the process. His later work largely focused on integrating existentialism and Marxism.

From the second half of the 20th century onward, Continental philosophy was largely interested in the ideas of Nietzsche and Heidegger, rather than the Cartesian principles of their ancestors. Metaphysics and rationalism were largely rejected at this stage, especially after the apocalyptic images provided during the World Wars. The specter of large-scale nuclear extermination made the West recoil in horror, believing the philosophies of the past to be at least partially responsible for the mass death of the 20th century.

However, despite the popularity of existentialism, in the 1950s, an anthropological movement, structuralism, sharply criticized the lack of empirical grounding in the popular philosophical movements. Beyond that, Sartre's involvement with the French Communist Party discredited his and related philosophies even further during the 1950s, when fear and suspicion of Communists ran rife through the United States and Western Europe.

Sartre, however, was not alone in his continued espousal of Marxist thought. Michel Foucault was particularly dedicated to the ultimate destruction of modern capitalist society. Son of a wealthy family of doctors in Poitiers, France, Foucault tried to hide the privilege into which he was born. Though he had a world-class education, Foucault felt quite different from his peers and began self-harming as a teen. Eventually seeking psychiatric care for his struggles, he was told that much of his mental anguish came from repressing his homosexuality and the burden that society placed on him to conceal his true self.

After reading Nietzsche's *Untimely Meditations*, Foucault realized that he wanted to be a philosophical historian in the vein of Nietzsche. Nietsche, like Kant, believed that there was something to be learned from the past, it was not a dry artifact to be studied from a distance. Foucault agreed with Nietzsche, and fiercely criticized many of the supposed advancements of Western society. Though it is typical for humanity to look back on the past with a condescending eye, Foucault did not. Instead, he argued that things like madness and capital punishment were more appropriately handled in the Renaissance and Middle Ages.

In the early 1960s, he published his first work, *Folie et déraison: histoire de la folie à l'âge classique (Madness and Unreason: A History of Madness in the Classical Age)* in which he harshly condemned the way that mentally ill people were treated from the 17th century onward. He argued that the over-medicalization of mental illness–separating people from their families, drugging, and institutionalizing them–though seen as more humane, was actually far worse than when they were allowed to freely roam society during the Renaissance. Similarly, he critiqued modern medicine as a whole, the modern prison system, and modern attitudes towards sex and sexuality. Though humanity likes to think progress is always linearly forward with time, Foucault disagreed and believed that it was worthwhile to study and look to the past for wisdom.

Overall, Foucault, like many of his peers, was disinterested in metaphysics, and the search for one ultimate truth. His work on systems of power and how power and knowledge interact, seen in books like *The History of Sexuality*, have remained relevant well into the 21st century.

Like Foucault, Jacques Derrida harbored similar derision for metaphysics. Born into a Jewish family in French-controlled Algeria, Derrida subsequently moved to Paris to continue his education. He was intimately familiar with being an outsider and a recipient of bigotry, both as a Jewish person and as an Algerian living in France, but he later achieved a great deal of popularity and acclaim in his professional life, much like Sartre had enjoyed a generation earlier.

Derrida is best remembered for his concept of deconstruction, which in short, refers to the destruction of blind loyalty to a concept or idea and a willingness to seek truth within the ideas that might oppose it. With this deconstructionist approach, Derrida looked at Western philosophy over the years and concluded that the field was guilty of false dichotomies since the time of Socrates. He pointed this out by demonstrating that within the field of philosophy, speech was often favored over writing. Expanding this out to civilization as a whole, he saw a vast number of things that were privileged over another in this way, in particular, the advancement of reason over passion or of men over women.

By valuing one thing over another, Western society, in Derrida's eyes, had discarded thoughts and ideas that had merit and value, and these supposedly "lesser" things deserved attention. The tendency for Western society to operate in a binary was unhelpful–to Derrida, everything has something that can be deemed useful, helpful, or otherwise important. Derrida was not interested in advancing any political agenda, but rather he was devoted to reminding people that life is messy and imperfect. No idea, person, or thing exists that has all the right answers. He proposed that people look at things more intelligently, seeing them all as shades of gray rather than as black and white opposites.

Derrida also pointed out that the metaphysical quest for totality, that is the quest for uncovering concepts like "goodness," "truth," or "reason," was behind the evil of totalitarianism. As he notes in his 1967 essay "Violence and Metaphysics,"

> *Incapable of respecting the Being and meaning of the other, phenomenology and ontology would be philosophies of violence. Through them, the entire philosophical tradition...would make common cause with oppression and technico-political possession.*

Emmanuel Lévinas (1905 - 1995 CE), another French philosopher, supported Derrida's assertions, pointing out that the consistent desire for totality was harmful, imposing a kind of dominion over the world and rewarding sameness attempting to destroy anything different in others. Following the work of Lévinas, philosophy in the modern era has looked to solve specific socio-political issues rather than answer broad questions. Yet, at the root of them all is the same soft wonder that accompanied the Greeks. Why are we here and what are we doing?

Western philosophy began as a quest to unravel life's greatest mysteries and answer the deepest questions about man's very existence. Though the idea of universal truth or good is largely ignored in modern times in favor of more granular political or social quandaries, philosophy remains a vehicle through which human existence in all of its forms is examined.

However much this field of wisdom advances though, it fails to sufficiently answer the great question of why humanity exists in the first place. Many have put forth ideas that range from meaningful to meaningless, but in the end, no one answer satisfies all people, and perhaps this is the beauty of philosophy. Time will continue, and theories will abound, but the answer to why we exist will continue to elude us.

I sincerely hope you enjoyed *A Brief History of Western Philosophy*. Reviews are a great way to share with others how you found the book and help me improve future books. **I would be grateful if you could take a minute to leave a review on Amazon.**

To leave a review, go to:

https://www.amazon.com/review/create-review?%20&asin=B0BT6RSQFF

Or scan with your camera

OTHER BOOKS BY DOMINIC HAYNES

(AVAILABLE ON AMAZON & AUDIBLE)

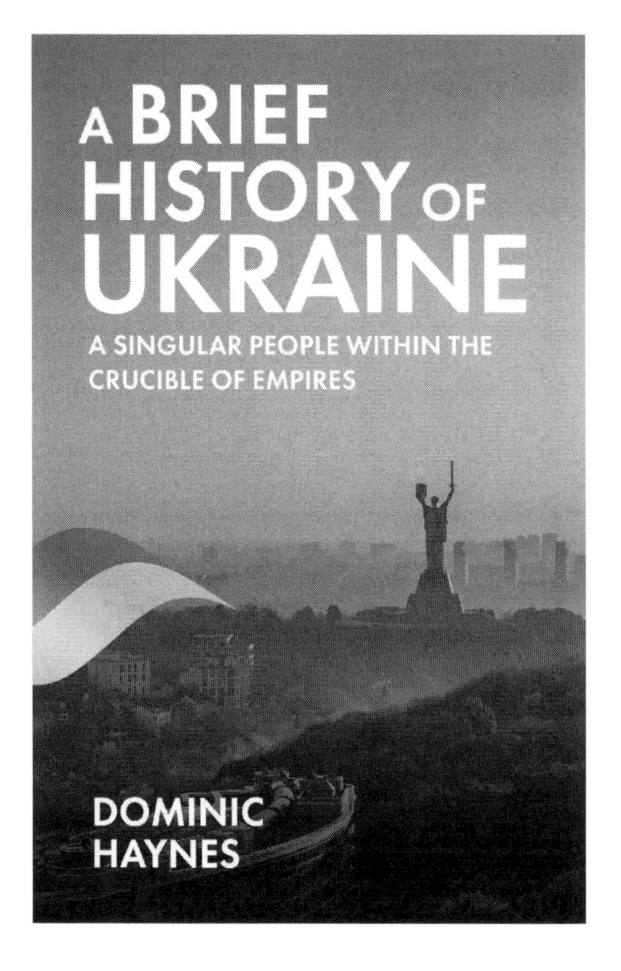

A Brief History of Ukraine: A Singular People Within the Crucible of Empires

A BRIEF HISTORY OF CANADA

HOW THE CLASH OF FRENCH, BRITISH AND NATIVE EMPIRES FORGED A UNIQUE IDENTITY

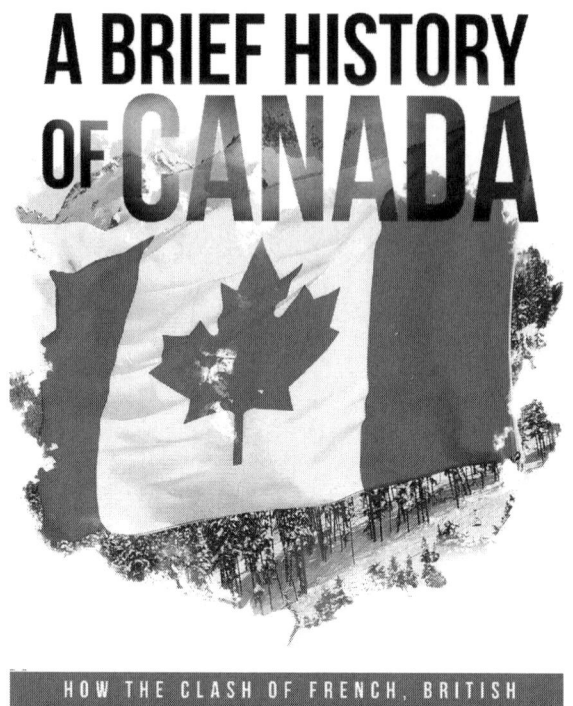

DOMINIC HAYNES

A Brief History of Canada: How the Clash of French, British and Native Empires Forged a Unique Identity

A BRIEF HISTORY OF AMERICA

CONTRADICTIONS & DIVISIONS IN THE UNITED STATES FROM THE REVOLUTIONARY ERA TO PRESENT DAY

DOMINIC HAYNES

A Brief History of America: Contradictions & Divisions in the United States from the Revolutionary Era to the Present Day

A BRIEF HISTORY OF ENGLAND

TRACING THE CROSSROADS OF CULTURES AND CONFLICTS FROM THE CELTS TO THE MODERN ERA

DOMINIC HAYNES

A Brief History of England: Tracing the Crossroads of Cultures and Conflicts from the Celts to the Modern Era

REFERENCES

Amadio, A. H. and Kenny, . Anthony J.P. (2021, March 2). *Aristotle*. *Encyclopedia Britannica*. https://www.britannica.com/biography/Aristotle

Ambury, J. (n.d.). *Socrates*. Internet Encyclopedia of Philosophy. https://iep.utm.edu/socrates/

Anschutz, R. Paul (2022, May 16). *John Stuart Mill*. *Encyclopedia Britannica*. https://www.britannica.com/biography/John-Stuart-Mill

Bargebuhr, F. P. (2021, June 13). *Ibn Gabirol*. *Encyclopedia Britannica*. https://www.britannica.com/biography/Ibn-Gabirol

Berryman, S. (2016, December 2). *Democritus*. Stanford Encyclopedia of Philosophy. https://plato.stanford.edu/entries/democritus/

Berryman, S. (2016, December 2). *Leucippus*. Stanford Encyclopedia of Philosophy. https://plato.stanford.edu/entries/leucippus/

Biletzki, A. and Matar, A. (2021, October 20). *Ludwig Wittgenstein*. Stanford Encyclopedia of Philosophy. https://plato.stanford.edu/entries/wittgenstein/

Bird, O. Allen and Duignan, . Brian (2022, April 18). *Immanuel Kant*. *Encyclopedia Britannica*. https://www.britannica.com/biography/Immanuel-Kant

Britannica, T. Editors of Encyclopaedia (2017, June 19). *Cyrenaic. Encyclopedia Britannica.* https://www.britannica.com/topic/Cyrenaic

Britannica, T. Editors of Encyclopaedia (2021, October 31). *G. E. Moore. Encyclopedia Britannica.* https://www.britannica.com/biography/G-E-Moore

Britannica, T. Editors of Encyclopaedia (2022, July 11). *Jacques Derrida. Encyclopedia Britannica.* https://www.britannica.com/biography/Jacques-Derrida

Britannica, T. Editors of Encyclopaedia (2022, January 1). *John Scotus Erigena. Encyclopedia Britannica.* https://www.britannica.com/biography/John-Scotus-Erigena

Britannica, T. Editors of Encyclopaedia (2010, August 10). *Liberal arts. Encyclopedia Britannica.* https://www.britannica.com/topic/liberal-arts

Britannica, T. Editors of Encyclopaedia (2022, January 10). *Megarian school. Encyclopedia Britannica.* https://www.britannica.com/topic/Megarian-school

Britannica, T. Editors of Encyclopaedia (2022, August 7). *Nicholas Of Cusa. Encyclopedia Britannica.* https://www.britannica.com/biography/Nicholas-of-Cusa

Britannica, T. Editors of Encyclopaedia (2017, June 14). *Parmenides. Encyclopedia Britannica.* https://www.britannica.com/biography/Parmenides-Greek-philosopher

Britannica, T. Editors of Encyclopaedia (2016, November 2). *Platonic Academy*. *Encyclopedia Britannica*. https://www.britannica.com/topic/Platonic-Academy

Britannica, T. Editors of Encyclopaedia (2021, October 5). *Robert Grosseteste*. *Encyclopedia Britannica*. https://www.britannica.com/biography/Robert-Grosseteste

Britannica, T. Editors of Encyclopaedia (2012, February 21). *Sextus Empiricus*. *Encyclopedia Britannica*. https://www.britannica.com/biography/Sextus-Empiricus

Britannica, T. Editors of Encyclopaedia (2021, November 11). *St. Albertus Magnus*. *Encyclopedia Britannica*. https://www.britannica.com/biography/Saint-Albertus-Magnus

Britannica, T. Editors of Encyclopaedia (2021, February 10). *Summa theologiae*. *Encyclopedia Britannica*. https://www.britannica.com/topic/Summa-theologiae

Britannica, T. Editors of Encyclopaedia (2022, April 19). *Thales of Miletus*. *Encyclopedia Britannica*. https://www.britannica.com/biography/Thales-of-Miletus

Britannica, T. Editors of Encyclopaedia (2018, March 9). *Thirty Tyrants*. *Encyclopedia Britannica*. https://www.britannica.com/topic/Thirty-Tyrants

Britannica, T. Editors of Encyclopaedia (2020, April 23). *voluntarism*. *Encyclopedia Britannica*. https://www.britannica.com/topic/voluntarism-philosophy

Britannica, T. Editors of Encyclopaedia (2020, April 23). *Zeno of Elea.* *Encyclopedia Britannica.* https://www.britannica.com/biography/Zeno-of-Elea

Calogero, G. and Starkey, Lawrence H. (2019, August 7). *Eleaticism.* *Encyclopedia Britannica.* https://www.britannica.com/topic/Eleaticism

Cambell, G. (n.d.). *Empedocles.* Internet Encyclopedia of Philosophy. https://iep.utm.edu/empedocles/

DeLong, J. (n.d.). *Parmenides.* Internet Encyclopedia of Philosophy. https://iep.utm.edu/parmenid/

Denova, R. (2022, March 25). *Augustine of Hippo.* World History Encyclopedia. https://www.worldhistory.org/Augustine_of_Hippo/

Desan, W. (2022, June 17). *Jean-Paul Sartre. Encyclopedia Britannica.* https://www.britannica.com/biography/Jean-Paul-Sartre

Desmet, R. and Irvine, A. (2018, September 4). *Alfred North Whitehead.* Stanford Encyclopedia of Philosophy. https://plato.stanford.edu/entries/whitehead/#Meta

Diano, C. (2019, August 8). *Epicurus. Encyclopedia Britannica.* https://www.britannica.com/biography/Epicurus

Dutton, B. (n.d.). *Benedict de Spinoza (1632 - 1677).* Internet Encyclopedia of Philosophy. https://iep.utm.edu/spinoza/#SH3a

REFERENCES | 169

Duke, G. (n.d.). *The Sophists (Ancient Greece)*. Internet Encyclopedia of Philosophy. https://iep.utm.edu/sophists/

Faubion, J. (2022, June 21). *Michel Foucault. Encyclopedia Britannica*. https://www.britannica.com/biography/Michel-Foucault

Flage, D. (n.d.). *George Berkeley (1685 - 1753)*. Internet Encyclopedia of Philosophy. https://iep.utm.edu/george-berkeley-british-empiricist/

Flannery, M. (2022, April 11). *Avicenna. Encyclopedia Britannica*. https://www.britannica.com/biography/Avicenna

Graham, D. (n.d.). *Anaximenes*. Internet Encyclopedia of Philosophy. https://iep.utm.edu/anaximenes/

Grief, I. (2021, August 18). *Boethius: First of the Medievals?*. World History Encyclopedia. https://www.worldhistory.org/article/1804/boethius-first-of-the-medievals/

Helden, A. Van (2022, June 14). *Galileo. Encyclopedia Britannica*. https://www.britannica.com/biography/Galileo-Galilei

Hildebrand, D. (2018, November 1). *John Dewey*. Stanford Encyclopedia of Philosophy. https://plato.stanford.edu/entries/dewey

History.com, Editors. (2021, October 29). *Aristotle*. History.com. https://www.history.com/topics/ancient-history/aristotle

Hübscher, A. (2022, February 18). *Arthur Schopenhauer. Encyclopedia Britannica*. https://www.britannica.com/biography/Arthur-Schopenhauer

170 | REFERENCES

Huffman, C. (2018). *Pythagoras*. Stanford Encyclopedia of Philosophy. https://plato.stanford.edu/entries/pythagoras

Irvine, A. (2020, May 27). *Bertrand Russell*. Stanford Encyclopedia of Philosophy. https://plato.stanford.edu/entries/russell/

Jorati, J. (n.d.). *Gottfried Liebniz: Philosophy of the Mind*. Internet Encyclopedia of Philosophy. https://iep.utm.edu/lei-mind/

Kroner, R. (2022, May 15). *Johann Gottlieb Fichte. Encyclopedia Britannica*. https://www.britannica.com/biography/Johann-Gottlieb-Fichte

Lawler, L. and Moulard-Leonard, V. (2021, July 3). *Henri Bergson*. Stanford Encyclopedia of Philosophy. https://plato.stanford.edu/entries/bergson/#ConcMult

Lendering, J. (2020, September 22). *Seven Sages*. Livius. https://www.livius.org/articles/people/seven-sages/

Levi, A. William , Wolin, . Richard , Fritz, . Kurt von , Stroll, . Avrum , Chambre, . Henri , Maurer, . Armand and McLellan, . David T. (2021, January 28). *Western philosophy. Encyclopedia Britannica*. https://www.britannica.com/topic/Western-philosophy

Levin, J. (2018, July 20). *Functionalism*. Stanford Encylopedia of Philosophy. https://plato.stanford.edu/entries/functionalism/

Longworth, G. (2021, June 30). *John Langshaw Austin*. Stanford Encyclopedia of Philosophy. https://plato.stanford.edu/entries/austin-jl/

REFERENCES | 171

Look, B. C. and Belaval, Yvon (2022, June 27). *Gottfried Wilhelm Leibniz.* *Encyclopedia Britannica.* https://www.britannica.com/biography/Gottfried-Wilhelm-Leibniz

Luscombe, D. Edward (2022, April 17). *Peter Abelard. Encyclopedia Britannica.* https://www.britannica.com/biography/Peter-Abelard

Magnus, B. (2022, August 21). Friedrich Nietzsche. Encyclopedia Britannica. https://www.britannica.com/biography/Friedrich-Nietzsche

Mansfield, H. (2022, June 17). *Niccolò Machiavelli. Encyclopedia Britannica.* https://www.britannica.com/biography/Niccolo-Machiavelli

Mark, J. (2021, May 26). *Democritus.* World History Encyclopedia. https://www.worldhistory.org/Democritus/

Mark, J. (2022, May 6). *French Wars of Religion.* World History Encyclopedia. https://www.worldhistory.org/French_Wars_of_Religion/

Mark, J. (2022, February 24). *Gorgias.* World History Encyclopedia. https://www.worldhistory.org/Gorgias/

Mark, J. (2019, May 23). *Pythagoras.* World History Encyclopedia. https://www.worldhistory.org/Pythagoras/

Mark, J. (2009, September 2). *Socrates.* World History Encyclopedia. https://www.worldhistory.org/socrates/

Markie, P. and Folescu, M. (2021, September 2). *Rationalism vs. Empiricism.* Stanford Encyclopedia of Philosophy. https://plato.stanford.edu/entries/rationalism-empiricism/

172 | REFERENCES

Machamer, P. and Miller, D. (2021, June 1). *Galileo Galilei*. Stanford Encyclopedia of Philosophy. https://plato.stanford.edu/entries/galileo/

Mojsisch, B and Summerell, O. (2011, April 25). *Meister Eckhart*. Stanford Encyclopedia of Philosophy. https://plato.stanford.edu/entries/meister-eckhart/#2

Nadler, S. (2020, April 16). *Baruch Spinoza*. Stanford Encyclopedia of Philosophy. https://plato.stanford.edu/entries/spinoza/#GodNatu

Naess, A. D. and Wolin, . Richard (2022, May 22). *Martin Heidegger*. Encyclopedia Britannica. https://www.britannica.com/biography/Martin-Heidegger-German-philosopher

Nails, D. and Monoson, S. (2022, May 26). *Socrates*. Stanford Encyclopedia of Philosophy. https://plato.stanford.edu/entries/socrates/

Palmer, J. (2020, October 19). *Parmenides*. Stanford Encyclopedia of Philosophy. https://plato.stanford.edu/entries/parmenides/#ModInt

Patzia, M. (n.d.). *Xenophanes*. Internet Encyclopedia of Philosophy. https://iep.utm.edu/xenoph/

Philosopher Anaximenes: Theory & Quotes. (2017, January 30). Study.com https://study.com/academy/lesson/philosopher-anaximenes-theory-quotes-quiz.html

Platanakis, C. (2018, February 4). *Cynic*. Encyclopedia Britannica. https://www.britannica.com/topic/Cynic-ancient-Greek-philosophy

Quinn, J. Francis (2022, July 11). *Saint Bonaventure. Encyclopedia Britannica.* https://www.britannica.com/biography/Saint-Bonaventure

Ramsey, W. (2019, March 11). *Eliminative Materialism.* Stanford Encyclopedia of Philosophy. https://plato.stanford.edu/entries/materialism-eliminative/

Rosenthal, E. I.J. (2022, January 1). *Averroës. Encyclopedia Britannica.* https://www.britannica.com/biography/Averroes

Saner, H. (2022, February 22). *Karl Jaspers. Encyclopedia Britannica.* https://www.britannica.com/biography/Karl-Jaspers

Schürmann, R. (2020, January 8). *Meister Eckhart. Encyclopedia Britannica.* https://www.britannica.com/biography/Meister-Eckhart

Smith, D. (2013, December 16). *Phenomenology.* Stanford Encyclopedia of Philosophy. https://plato.stanford.edu/entries/phenomenology/

Sorell, T. (2022, May 16). *Thomas Hobbes. Encyclopedia Britannica.* https://www.britannica.com/biography/Thomas-Hobbes

Spade, P. (2019, March 5). *William of Ockham.* Stanford Encyclopedia of Philosophy. https://plato.stanford.edu/entries/ockham/

Tanney, J. (2021, May 12). *Gilbert Ryle.* Stanford Encyclopedia of Philosophy. https://plato.stanford.edu/entries/ryle/

Urbach, P. Michael , Lea, . Kathleen Marguerite , Quinton, . Anthony M. and Quinton, . Baron (2022, April 18). *Francis Bacon. Encyclopedia*

Britannica. https://www.britannica.com/biography/Francis-Bacon-Viscount-Saint-Alban

Vignaux, P. D. (2021, May 9). *William of Ockham*. Encyclopedia Britannica. https://www.britannica.com/biography/William-of-Ockham

Wasson, D. (2020, September 22). *René Descartes*. World History Encyclopedia. https://www.worldhistory.org/Rene_Descartes/

Watson, R. A. (2022, March 27). *René Descartes. Encyclopedia Britannica.* https://www.britannica.com/biography/Rene-Descartes

Westphal, M. (2022, May 1). *Søren Kierkegaard. Encyclopedia Britannica.* https://www.britannica.com/biography/Soren-Kierkegaard

Williams, T. (2019, October 11). *John Duns Scotus*. Stanford Encyclopedia of Philosophy. https://plato.stanford.edu/entries/duns-scotus/

Printed in Great Britain
by Amazon